CW00351020

e-Business

a jargon-free practical guide

e-Business

a jargon-free practical guide

J. A. Matthewson

OXFORD   AUCKLAND   BOSTON   JOHANNESBURG   MELBOURNE   NEW DELHI

Butterworth-Heinemann
Linacre House, Jordan Hill, Oxford OX2 8DP
225 Wildwood Avenue, Woburn, MA 01801-2041
A division of Reed Educational and Professional Publishing Ltd

℞ A member of the Reed Elsevier plc group

First published 2002

© J. A. Matthewson 2002

All rights reserved. No part of this publication may be reproduced in
any material form (including photocopying or storing in any medium by
electronic means and whether or not transiently or incidentally to some
other use of this publication) without the written permission of the
copyright holder except in accordance with the provisions of the Copyright,
Designs and Patents Act 1988 or under the terms of a licence issued by the
Copyright Licensing Agency Ltd, 90 Tottenham Court Road, London,
England W1P 0LP. Applications for the copyright holder's written
permission to reproduce any part of this publication should be addressed
to the publishers

TRADEMARKS/REGISTERED TRADEMARKS
Computer hardware and software brand names mentioned in this book are
protected by their respective trademarks and are acknowledged.

British Library Cataloguing in Publication Data
A catalogue record for this book is available from the British Library

Library of Congress Cataloguing in Publication Data
A catalogue record for this book is available from the Library of Congress

ISBN 0 7506 5293 4

For information on all Butterworth-Heinemann publications visit our
website at: **www.bh.com**

 Designed and typeset by Elle and P.K. McBride, Southampton

Printed and bound in Great Britain

FOR EVERY TITLE THAT WE PUBLISH, BUTTERWORTH-HEINEMANN
WILL PAY FOR BTCV TO PLANT AND CARE FOR A TREE.

Contents

CONTENTS

Foreword

This book is long overdue. The world of e-business is increasingly complicated by the array of acronyms and technical terms in daily use that baffle anyone who is not fully conversant with the equipment and processes that underpin electronic business methods. At last, here is a useful management guide to e-business processes and practice that cuts out the jargon and explains in clear, concise language and graphics how to plan, implement, market and manage an e-business enterprise. There are handy hints and tips, examples and case studies that illustrate the theory and put e-business methods into practice and perspective.

One of the biggest challenges for e-business companies is communication: communication with customers, partners, industry bodies and the press. Yet as with most complex processes, it's not necessary to understand every technical term and function, only to understand how these functions fit together to form a business process. For instance, most of us wear a wristwatch or drive a car without understanding the mechanics of the technology. e-Business is no different. It's not about Internet usage, the Web, access devices or backend technology, although these are all issues that must be addressed. Neither is it about venture capital and brand building. The rules have changed.

What counts now is cash flow and profitability, just like any traditional business. What's happening is that electronic business methods are being absorbed into mainstream business practice. There's no such thing anymore as an Internet company, there are only businesses that employ electronic sales, communication and service channels. In a few years, all businesses will have an e-business dimension.

That's where e-business is going, and as a practical guide, James Matthewson has written an invaluable handbook for students, managers and anyone else who wants or needs to know more about this essential and fascinating subject.

Mark Simpson
Commercial Manager
IMRG, interactive media in retail group
www.imrg.org

Acknowledgements

I am not a deeply religious man, but firstly, I thank God for giving me the strength and ability to write this book, and for everything else I am able to do. I also want to thank my wife Melanie for keeping me on the straight and narrow while writing – a difficult task, my dog Jasper for insisting on those long and thoughtful walks in the Surrey countryside, and my team at shrinking earth.net, for their continued commitment to reading. To Delia, my Editor, thank you for your patience and for believing in me. To the rest of the BH team, thank you also for a great job. And, finally to you to the reader. Thank you for choosing this book and e-business as an interest or career. We are not there by any means yet, but soon. Soon.

James Matthewson

 **Preface**

Do you wear a wristwatch? If you do, wear it on your other wrist for the duration of reading this book. Feel strangely uncomfortable? Good, because that's how e-business should feel when you do it. Why? I'll explain later.

On my travels, I regularly get asked: "What is e-business?" A difficult question to answer: one that is complex; specific and unique to the enquirer's own business at that time and something that is completely open to interpretation. So, I've written this book. It's designed to help business and marketing students, practitioners and anyone else interested, develop their e-business strategy. In this book, we'll cut through the hype, the myths and stick to the facts. Plain and simple, jargon-free and practical. By the end of this book, you will be in a position to develop your own e-business plan, I promise.

So how does it all start? Well, in order to develop your e-business strategy, you must first understand the primary issues that face today's business and marketer.

Adopting e-business developments (at work and at home)

While the UK and European market currently sits behind the USA in its adoption of e-business, Europe will form the next frontier for e-business growth in the coming three years. e-Business will affect work and home life in all sorts of ways and at all sorts of times. People – you – will change your attitude to work, life and the way you buy.

How will e-business evolve?

In this book, we'll look at how growth in the adoption of alternatives to the PC for accessing the Internet will accelerate user adoption, in all aspects of everyday work and home life. Today, home Internet usage exceeds business usage, in the number of access points, due mainly to restrictive practices within the working environment. But factors such as the introduction of new Internet access devices, falling PC prices, free Internet access through service providers such as FreeServe and the emergence of higher speed data transmission capabilities (called *broadband*), will mean continued growth in home and work access.

A good example of the Internet's impact on home and work life can be found in the town of Ennis, Ireland. In 1997, the entire village was connected to the Internet and a local Intranet was set-up to establish connections between its community and local businesses. Since then, the technology has impacted on every aspect of village life, with 82 per cent of homes now Internet-enabled and 40 per cent of businesses trading online; All primary and secondary students, and their teachers now have their own e-mail address and a Visa

Cash rechargeable smart card allows users to buy goods at retail outlets and pay and display car parks – WAP technology then allows the user to top up their Visa card with their mobile phones. e-Business is enhancing home and business life, everyday, everywhere.

But where are we now? – hype vs reality

To survive in this new economy, it is no longer enough to have a brilliant idea to gain funding and make an Internet-based business model succeed. Recent stock market plunges have left dozens of Internet companies near-broke and desperate for a survival miracle. For some, that means a quick sell-out or an accelerated merger deal. For others, it means restructuring their plans, shutdowns and redundancies. Most important, newcomers to the Internet space have to work even harder to prove themselves to investors than those during the early goldrush. An e-business must show potential for profitability in the short-term – typically this has been part of the strategy that was overlooked. Consequently, e-businesses with a year or so behind them are cancelling or postponing IPOs while navel-gazing their futures.

So, whether *you* are B2B or B2C, it won't matter anymore. The rules of e-business have changed and successful e-businesses will be based on what all traditional business models have been based on – cash flow and profitability, not intangible brand building goals. If you are a traditional business looking to harness the power of the Internet, then you have a head start, with existing customers, strong relationships with suppliers and channels.

Assessing the viability of *your* e-business requires you to look well beyond the current market and focus on the next three to five years. Sustainability in your business model will be critical including those important factors such as customers, cash and competition.

What are the key business issues YOU face?

If you intend to do e-business, which I assume you do, you will come to realize that there are many business issues to be faced, overcome and learned from. The key questions and challenges facing you and your team include delivery. Can you do what you promise? Have you got the right business model? Are you moving from a traditional business to a new Internet-based business? Who are your customers? Where are they? What do they want from you? Is your brand strong enough? Does it have value? Do customers recognise you online? Are you organized properly for e-business?

Don't worry. We'll answer these questions as you go through the book.

e-Business technology – have you got it?

Commonly, I hear references to the five key technologies that are believed to underpin the future of e-business. These include sheer *computing* power that enables decision makers like you to analyze situations and develop solutions to complex problems. *Mobile technology* designed to offer your customers an 'anytime, anywhere' moment of interactivity with your e-business, primarily from non-PC devices. The emergence of wireless devices and Internet-appliances will facilitate the delivery of information to customers in cars, at home and through their clothes (for example, Gucci's Internet-enabled sunglasses).

Sensing technologies will identify the location of customers wherever they are using products and services in the new world – these will be particularly important to the success of mobile e-business (or m-commerce as it is known). The development of *increasing bandwidth* for accessing the network will enable new applications and drive Internet penetration. The market for universal access is very competitive, as witnessed by the recent telephony licence bidding wars across Europe. However, significant consolidation within the marketplace is likely to occur in the near future, raising questions over which groups of companies are well positioned to achieve market dominance in access to the Internet and, potentially, dominance in the industries they compete in.

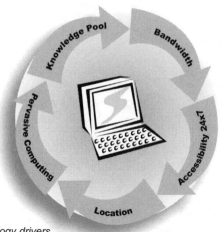

The key e-business technology drivers

The future in e-business. How will it look?

We are now seeing explosive growth in e-business, fuelled by hype, fear and confusion. Every day new business models emerge and research agencies predict scenarios that ensure the frenzy continues to run, for a while longer. So what will happen to you? By the time you've read this book, you'll be fuelled and ready to go with your e-business strategy. But which way will you go? Will your e-business strategy focus on making efficiency and cost reduction improvements in your offline business? Will your e-business strategy be to depend on and exist solely on online trading? Will your web site be the next big e-marketplace? So what will you do?

Read on, and all will be revealed. :-)

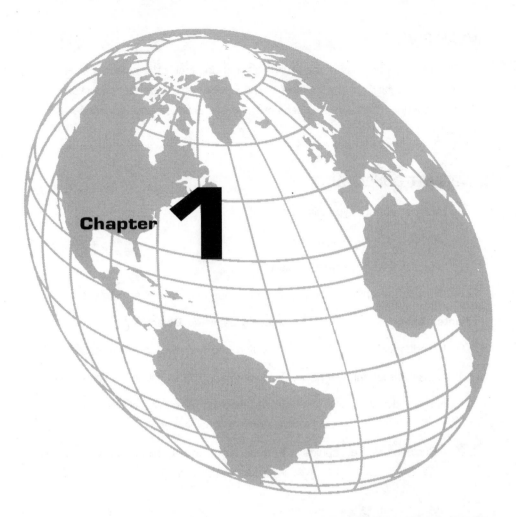

Chapter 1

Introducing
the fourth channel

OVERVIEW

This chapter introduces the fourth trading channel – the digital channel. It outlines the birth of the Internet and describes the benefits and risks of multi-channel marketing, to promote and sell products and services online.

LEARNING OBJECTIVES

In this first chapter you will learn:

- About the birth of e-business
- About the various new media channels
- How to use these channels in a business and marketing context

Chapter Topic	Specific Learning Objective
1.0 Introduction	To define and understand e-business
1.1 A brief historical overview	To understand the evolution of e-business
1.2 New media channels	To review each of the digital channels available to businesses
1.3 e-Business demographics	To understand who's online and the growth in channel adoption

KEYWORDS

e-business	EDI	eTokens	SMS
GSM	WAP	GPRS	iTV
Kiosks	Walled garden	Reach	Acquisition
Location-based marketing			

Notepad exercises: 3

1.0 Introduction

Simply put, new media is a combination of digital technologies that facilitate informational and transactional communications between two or more parties. If you think of new media as just the Internet, think again! New media is ubiquitous and an extremely personalized way of reaching content. Yes, much of the 'new media' talk we hear about relates to e-business – the process of making *business* transactions via a computer and some form of network - e.g. a direct connection or the Internet. This includes Business-to-Business (B2B) transactions, online retailing or Business-to-Consumer (B2C) and the digitalization of the financial industry, amongst many others.

> "e-Business is the relocation of internal and external business processes to the Internet."
>
> IBM

But new media goes beyond this. It encompasses the Internet, interactive TV (iTV), interactive kiosks, mobile devices such as WAP phones and Personal Digital Assistants (PDAs), games consoles, digital radio and eventually kitchen appliances, such as your microwave oven (well, maybe some day!). Some experts argue that e-business includes all the steps that occur in any business cycle, such as advertising, purchasing, invoicing and the delivery of customer support and services.

The term 'e-business', often used interchangeably with 'e-Business' or 'Internet business', covers a lot of ground and refers to all these areas. In this book, we will cover all this ground.

1.1 A brief historical overview

e-Business originally began in the 1970s, when large corporations started to create private networks that enabled them to share information with business partners and suppliers. This process, called Electronic Data Interchange (EDI), transmitted standardized data that streamlined the procurement process between businesses, so that paperwork and human intervention were nearly eliminated and human errors reduced.

EDI is Electronic Data Interchange – a set of standard protocols for conducting highly structured interorganization exchanges, such as for making purchases or initiating information requests.

EDI is very much in place and has become so effective at reducing costs and improving efficiency, that an estimated 95% of Fortune 1,000 companies use it. EDI was, and still is, the foundation of e-business. Today, e-business increasingly refers to business transactions conducted over the Internet. EDI, for example, is being brought to the Internet and allowing companies to save money by eliminating the old system and expensive private networks, and expand their reach to include more businesses in the supply chain. Other business-to-business transactions are simply moving to the Web without using the standardized forms required by EDI.

But much of the e-business buzz we hear about on the radio, see on TV and read about in the press refers to online retailing; that is, using the Internet and Web to sell goods, services and information to business and consumer customers. Online retailing began about four years ago, and was pioneered largely by Internet companies that didn't (and some still don't) perform traditional retail, such as Amazon.com, Dell and CDnow. More recently, brand names such as Virgin and British Airways have established fully transactional capabilities on the Internet, with experts believing that these and other brand names will develop a longlasting presence on the Web. Today, all an individual needs to shop online is a computer with a modem, a web-browser and Internet access through an Internet Service Provider and their standard telephone line or through a digital TV. He or she can then buy flowers, tickets, music, financial services and even cars.

To date, online retailers have had mixed results. Many businesses have failed to meet their revenue expectations and have learnt that setting-up an electronic shop on the web is a more complicated and costly exercise than predicted. Take the demise of boo.com for example, who in fewer than two years spent £100m in venture capital and couldn't generate the required income levels to sustain their business. We'll take at look at this in more detail in Chapter 11.

Additionally, traditional 'bricks and mortar' retail businesses have come late to the online world as they have lacked confidence in consumer adoption, the process of fulfilling online orders and managing security of customer data, specifically relating to credit card transactions. But there has been much success on the web. Recent research in the 'eEurope' report from eMarketer.com predicts that the number of active Internet users in Europe will grow from 70 million at the end of 2000, to 108 million by the end of this year, and 255 million by the end of 2004.

This increasing level of Internet use will drive e-business revenues in the region and cause the value of the total European e-business to rise to $68.9 billion by the end of 2001, which will be a 100 percent increase on 2000. That value should rise to $980 billion by 2004.

1.2 New media channels

Marketing and advertising is moving into a new dimension. The advent of interactive capabilities, delivered to the TV set, mobile phone, portable digital assistant, interactive kiosks and other devices will undoubtedly see selling and marketing taking place on one level. If your customers can interact with your content via different devices, they can just as easily buy.

Figure 1.1   Role of different channels and the customer, squarely at the centre

In this section we will explore new, interactive channels and discuss what these mean to YOU, the e-business-person and e-marketer. We will also look at the advantages and disadvantages of different digital channels and the key steps you should follow in integrating them into your e-business strategy.

The Wireless Internet

Technology is evolving at a rapid pace and it seems like only yesterday we were surrounded by hype announcing the launch of WAP and the 'mobile Internet'. But the mobile Internet comes in various guises: SMS, WAP, GPRS, iMode....what do all these mean? Let's take a look.

What is SMS?

Short Message Service (SMS) is the ability to send and receive text messages between mobile phones. Messages can be comprised of words, numbers or alpha-numeric combinations, but not graphics, sounds, animations or movies, yet!

SMS is part of the GSM phone standard. The first SMS message was believed to have been sent in late 1992 from a PC to a mobile phone on the Vodafone network.

GSM is the Global System for Mobile communication – the first truly international digital mobile communications standard of which there are 373 network providers operating across 161 countries. Global subscribers to GSM stood at 655 million at the end of December 2000.

SMS offers up to a maximum of 160 characters including spaces, meaning messages need to be crisp. For the creative marketer, SMS can be great for location-based initiatives, such as promotions that offer customers a discount if they take their mobile phone into your shop and show the SMS message received to the check-out using e-tokens.

Figure 1.2   The Vbox from Motorola – Designed for text messaging

FACTS & FIGURES   The mobile scene

- There will be over 1 billion mobile phone users worldwide by 2003 – Yankee Group
- Japan has more mobile phones than fixed phones
- Italy has more mobile phones than credit cards
- Approximately one third of mobile phones will be WAP enabled by 2003
- In the UK, mobile phone penetration has now reached 50% of the population and represents double that of Internet usage
- Ovum predict that by 2005, over 500 million mobile device users will engage in m-commerce
- According to Durlacher, European m-commerce will be worth an estimated Euro 24 billion by 2003, led by Italy, Germany and the UK
- Worldwide device sales of mobile phones will exceed 575 million units in 2001

Tip: e-Tokens are a simple but effective way of sending a promotion to a mobile phone using text messages.

INTRODUCING THE FOURTH CHANNEL

Location-based marketing is the method of targeting customers at a specific location and point in time using the mobile communications network as the delivery vehicle.

ADVANTAGES/DISADVANTAGES

SMS to e-business and e-marketing

Advantages

- It's ubiquitous – over 95% of mobile phone users can send and receive 'text' messages

- It's new, simple and an effective method of communications

- It's popular, particularly with the youth sector

Disadvantages

- It's limited to text only (160 characters including spaces)

- It lacks interactivity

- It's not transactional

- It offers limited measurability

CASE STUDY: ZAGME

Zagme is a WAP service-provider offering shoppers at two UK shopping centres (Bluewater and Lakeside) access to exclusive deals and offers direct to the mobile phone through SMS messaging. The service is free to users and is designed to enable shoppers to take advantage of offers whilst they are at the shopping centre. This uses 'location-based' marketing techniques by identifying the shopper as present at the centre through their connection to the cellular network. When a GSM mobile phone (accounting for 95% of mobile phones used in the UK) is connected to the cellular network, the handset and nearest base station communicate with each other via 'cells'. Each cell and base station has a location reference that enables services like ZagMe to target users with SMS messages when they are within the shopping centre location.

To learn more about Zagme, visit www.ZagMe.com.

CASE STUDY: BOLTBLUE

Boltblue's mobile solutions pumps up blood donations by 32%

The work of the National Blood Service saves thousands of lives each year. Traditionally blood donors are encouraged to donate by a mix of media messages from prime time TV commercials to posters at the local doctor's surgery. As people get older they are more likely to have had health problems that exclude them from donating, and after a certain age, they are no longer able to give at all. So the NBS is in continual need of 'fresh blood' and aims to target young people with a longer lifetime value. Whatever their age, when donors register their intention to give, the NBS maintains a dialogue with them using a series of mailings. Over the course of a year an individual can donate up to three times, so the mailings, although regular, are well spread out. In the life of a student, four months is a long time. Typically on arrival at university temporary accommodation is taken and somewhere more long-term found a few weeks in. Also, home visits between terms and seeing friends at other universities make students a very mobile bunch. And with under 6% of people in the country eligible to give blood actually donating the NBS wanted an effective way to communicate with this vital group.

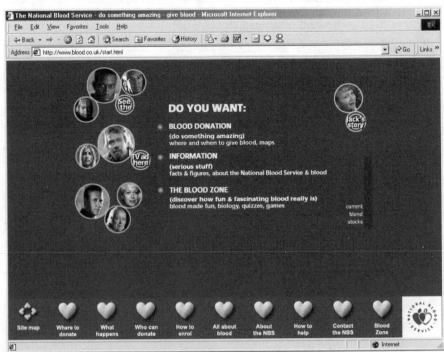

Figure 1.3 The National Blood Service web site

"For us the difficulty with the student population is not their willingness to donate, but their mobile lifestyles."

Martin Weller, Marketing Initiatives Manager for the National Blood Service.

Thanks to 'pay as you go' mobiles and high numbers of concerned parents wanting an easy way of contacting their offspring when studying, virtually every university student has a mobile phone. So, wherever they may be, their mobile phone is more likely than not to be with them.

Boltblue, the mobile portal and mobile business solutions company, knows students well. Its consumer portal (main site) has over 2 million registered users, mostly aged between 19 and 25, a high proportion of whom are students. Young people use the site to download a wide variety of content from news and travel to icons, ring tones and jokes. These are the group whose phone is more than a communications tool; it is a device for gathering vital information and an accessory which can be customised to express the personality of the user. Knowing this, Boltblue recognised that students would welcome requested messages from third parties so they approached the NBS and persuaded them to trial text messaging with a sample of university students in place of mail. The NBS agreed and arranged for their representatives to register the mobile phone numbers of the students of five UK universities at their freshers' fairs. Initially the NBS thought one text message would do as they had always sent one reminder postcard to registered students. Boltblue instead advised a series of messages to build a more sustained relationship and together Boltblue and the NBS crafted a series of catchy messages to be delivered over a period of time. The resulting four messages still came in at a fraction of the price of a stamp.

The Boltblue messages used the text messaging shorthand with which the target group were already familiar. And according to the time and place of each donor session registered students were invited to book an appointment by mobile. The response to this alone improved efficiency for the NBS. The added facility of booking a session by mobile ensured that the appointments were spread throughout the session and helped reduce the rush-hour bottlenecks that typically result when large numbers of donors arrive to donate at peak times. A mobile message was then sent confirming each individual's booking and another reminding each donor a day beforehand of the session was sent to their mobiles. The programme took place during the autumn storms and floods of 2000, and a number of the donor sessions had to be cancelled and rescheduled at short notice. Thanks to the use of mobiles the donors could be contacted by text and informed of the changes at high speed and low cost.

At the end of the trials the NBS recorded a 32% increase in donations from those that were communicated with via mobile means compared to those that weren't. In February 2001, the mobile communications programme was expanded to even more universities, on top of which viral marketing initiatives (see section 7.2) are running with more planned. Simple and effective but there was a spanner thrown in the works. Not a technology gremlin, but a meteorological one – the great British weather!

WAP – Wireless Application Protocol

It is suggested that by the end of 2001, all mobile phones sold in the UK will be capable of accessing the Internet.

This is achieved using a new communications protocol called WAP – Wireless Application Protocol – that enables a mobile phone user to access Internet style content whilst on the move. WAP-enabled phones will become more widespread as both businesses and consumers become increasingly attracted to these devices for their portability. Predictions by leading Internet research firm Forrester, state that there will be 41 million mobile users in the UK by 2005.

Yankee Group suggest that there will be over 1 billion mobile phone users worldwide by 2003.

These users will be split into two groups: multi-device users and single-device users. Multi-device users will have other means of going online apart from their phones, such as via their PCs, whilst single-device users will use the Internet only on their phones. It is predicted there will be 28 million multi-device users and 13 million single-device users in the UK by 2005.

As mobile network operators control the billing infrastructure, they will take advantage of this to become mobile e-business enablers. This will allow network operators such as Vodafone to offer customers the facility to purchase goods and services from their mobile phone and charge the transaction to their mobile phone account, to be reconciled and paid at the end of the month, rather than paying by credit card. However, revenue models for mobile e-business (m-commerce) will differ from that of traditional e-business. Customers are unlikely to browse the Internet for long periods at a time and will be unwilling to make complex purchases using their WAP phones. Successful companies will use 'trigger services' to attract WAP users to their offerings on all channels.

WAP is the standard designed to allow Internet content to be displayed on mobile devices, such as cell phones, personal organizers (PDAs) and pagers. The information is predominantly text-based to ensure rapid loading to the phone, but does include some small graphics. WAP provides the first building blocks to wireless marketing and is the logical next-step from SMS and the Internet evolution. WAP will become important to marketers, as it's the first technology that liberates the web from the desktop and allows customers to surf using 'pocket' browsers in handheld devices and cell phones.

The population of WAP users is growing, and more and more people are coming into the market now that WAP handsets are low-cost. It won't be too long before WAP becomes a standard handset feature.

A new breed of mobile phones has appeared called 'smart phones'. These include the functionality of PDAs plus WAP. Smart phones are getting smaller, quicker and cheaper!

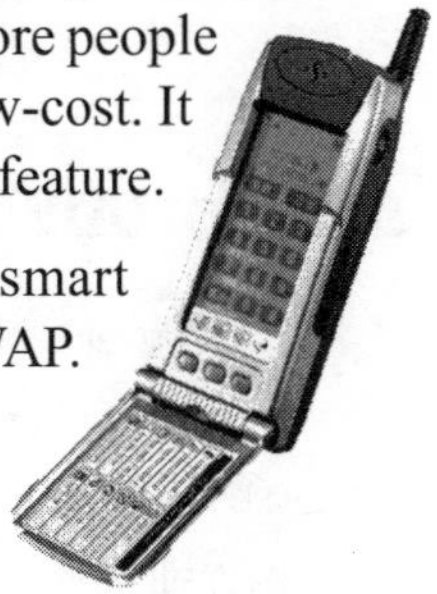

Figure 1.4   Smart phone from Samsung

ADVANTAGES/DISADVANTAGES

WAP to e-business and marketing

Advantages

- It's a new channel to market

- It's truly independent of time and space

- It's measurable (but see below)

- It's popular amongst the youth sector

Disadvantages

- It has limited penetration amongst mobile users currently

- It offers limited content delivery

- It lacks interactivity

- It's currently insecure, making it non-viable for e-business trading

- It's difficult to measure accurately

Low cost airline GO conducted a mobile advertising campaign in conjunction with mobile Internet portal Mviva. The advertising campaign incorporated using mobile ads (m-ads) delivered to WAP phones targeted at subscribers to the Mviva service. The objective of the campaign was to drive traffic to the

GO-fly web site to increase sales of low-cost flights, user registrations for their e-mail and SMS alert service and brand awareness of the GO brand. The campaign lasted two months and saw approximately 62,000 WAP phone users receive the m-ads through their connections to Mviva. It delivered a response of 14% (or 7000) click-throughs to the WAP site and a 27% increase in subscriptions to their e-mail and SMS alert services.

Figure 1.5   M-ads on Mviva by Go Airlines

CASE STUDY: BRITISH AIRWAYS

Customers of British Airways make over 40 million trips a year, of which, a large percentage are business customers who demand flexibility in their travel plans. e-Business has become a critical aspect of British Airways' overall business strategy. Their web site, at www.britishairways.com serves over 5000 individual web pages and provides content in 33 different languages in 92 countries. The site attracts over 3.5 million visits per months and generates around £1m in sales revenue per week. BA launched a new e-business solution designed to operate across other channels than just the web, but also integrated digital television, WAP, SMS and personal digital assistants. The integration of these channels was seen as critical to the success of their e-business strategy.

Figure 1.6   The British Airways WAP Flight Information Service

Due to the varying nature of BA's customer audience, it became apparent that different audiences had different information needs – business travellers it seemed, wanted to be able to change their travel plans at a moment's notice. This is where mobile channels came into their own for

BA. British Airways did some research and identified that 74% of business travellers take a laptop computer with them; 36% use a PDA and 92% use / own a mobile phone with a third of those using SMS and 14% using WAP services. Working with IBM, BA built a WAP service enabling customers to gain access to flight information and electronic check-in via their mobile telephones. The service provides real-time flight and departure information, seat allocations and a check-in facility. Customer service research has shown that 78% of BA customers who use the service considered it either 'good' or 'excellent'.

NOTEPAD EXERCISE

Jot down five ways in which you think you could use WAP to market and sell your products or services to customers. Then, list the key things your customers would find useful from you whilst they are on the move.

GPRS – General Packet Radio Service

Coming later this year is GPRS – General Purpose Radio System. It is hoped that it will change the way mobile Internet users will interact with the web. For a start, the mobile Internet device will be permanently connected to the Internet, removing the need to connect to perform functions and the concerns over cost. Second, GPRS is 'high bandwidth', meaning that web-style content access through mobile devices will be more like the web content accessed via the desk-top computer using a browser (e.g. pictures, videos, audio, animations and more).

The introduction of GPRS will offer e-business brands significant opportunities such as being able to deliver highly targeted advertising messages to customers whilst they are on the move.

ADVANTAGES OF GPRS

- **Increases data rates** by about 3–4 times – offering speeds of around 20–24Kbps.

- **Permanently connected** to the network, so information flows to and from the handset almost instantaneously.

- **Integrates e-mail** and other online applications.

- Introduces **location-based** marketing.

Location-based marketing will become a key targeted element of mobile commerce with customers requiring more versatile content, such as video, audio and animations. There are no definite cost guidelines currently on how much it will cost to use GPRS marketing, but as the technology moves on, this will become clear.

The future of the mobile Internet

Whilst WAP is useful now, the mobile Internet will evolve over the next few years in key areas such as speed, hardware (such as screen quality and battery life) and applications. In 2002/3, new systems will arrive like Universal Mobile Telecommunication System (UMTS) which, like GPRS, will move data around in packets, giving an 'Always On' functionality, but at higher speed.

USEFUL WEB SITES	Mobile business and marketing
Wireless Advertising Industry Association:	www.adforce.com/waia/
WAP Forum:	www.wapforum.org
Cellular Telecommunications Industry Assn.:	www.wow-com.com
Wireless Data Forum:	www.wirelessdata.org
Wireless Foundation:	www.wirelessfoundation.org

Interactive digital TV (iTV)

Interactive television is a new transmission system that uses computer technology instead of standard signals. It converts sound and pictures into computerised digits, which are transmitted through the air by modified transmitters. The digits can be received by standard aerials, satellite dishes or by cable, but have to be decoded and turned into sound or vision. This is done either with a separate set-top box, or a decoder built-in to your television (an 'integrated' TV set).

What does iTV mean?

Interactive TV basically means the availability of many more television channels than ever before, each with a consistent quality of pictures and crystal clear sound. It also introduces interactive services, such as on-screen shopping, banking, Internet access and e-mail. Interactive television will change the way your customers use their TV sets, enabling them to have a more interactive and rich experience with your brand through the TV set, over conventional TV advertising and sponsorship, all via a remote control.

Figure 1.7   Interactive TV from Open

NOTEPAD EXERCISE

Jot down five ways in which you think you could use interactive TV to market and sell your products or services to customers.

ADVANTAGES/DISADVANTAGES

Interactive TV

Advantages

- **It makes you accessible** – customers can access the products and services they want through the universality of television and the familiarity of the remote control

- **It's user-friendly** – simple, intuitive navigation

- **It's mass market** – the TV set is ubiquitous

- **It's secure** – safe and private place to trade

- **It's Interactive** - complete purchase environment

Disadvantages

- **It's not the Web** – content must be 're-purposed' (See Chapter 7)

- **It's a 'walled-garden'** – not a standard, open system

- **It's in its infancy** – Only 10m UK homes currently have it

- **It's expensive** – implementation costs are high

INTRODUCING THE FOURTH CHANNEL

Applications of iTV to e-business & e-marketing

- Advertising
- e-Mail and text information services
- Electronic programming guides
- Interacting with TV shows (e-gaming)
- Home shopping, including banking.

3 Key steps to achieving iTV reality

1.   Start Small – deploying all your content and ads on iTV can be very expensive. Start by testing small amounts of advertising inventory on programme guides or other non-competitive content areas to see what reaction is gained from your target audience.

2.   Develop an iTV site – having tested iTV ads that drive traffic to your web site or call centre, the next step is to develop your own content area on iTV within a *'walled garden'* that your ads will deliver traffic to. This is similar to developing a web site. See Section 7.5 on content repurposing for further information.

Tip: A walled-garden is the term used to describe an area where the content is owned and controlled by a specific platform provider. For example, the content available has been designed only for the TV platform and doesn't offer full Internet browsing capabilities. A good example of a walled garden on the Internet is AOL's site.

3.   Grow your offer – from delivering content, offers and advertising through your iTV channel, the next stage is to begin integrating other services such as purchasing, e-mail, personalization etc. Note: this is where iTV get really expensive.

The Internet kiosk

In over 10,000 UK locations you can find an interactive kiosk connected to the Internet. Typically found in shopping centres, airports and train stations (anywhere with heavy footfall), interactive Internet kiosks are providing companies with the opportunity to communicate, sell to and capture information from customers on the move. Kiosks are also used for sending and receiving e-mail, locating accommodation, bars and restaurants and places of interest.

Interactive kiosks are one of the most versatile and cost-effective marketing tools available. Compact and robust, the can be placed virtually anywhere that attracts passing footfall of customers. Interactive kiosks can also take many forms, from stunning design-led units to more practical, engineered units that are almost impossible to ignore. This makes them ideal not just for sales and marketing, but public information purposes and corporate communications. So how can you use interactive kiosks as part of your marketing communications and e-marketing strategy?

Figure 1.8   An interactive kiosk design for beeb.com

ADVANTAGES/DISADVANTAGES

Interactive kiosks

Advantages

- Multipurpose, multimedia devices that act as a focus of attention
- Extend *reach* to passing footfall customers
- Capture data from interested customers
- Can be free standing and un-attended
- Can be integrated with the Internet or your own office network

Disadvantages

- Can be expensive
- Require maintenance contracts and support
- Can be subject to vandalism

NOTEPAD EXERCISE

Write down some ways in which you could use iKiosks as part of your e-business and e-marketing strategy, and where you would use them.

Kiosks can be used for entertaining, informing or selling to customers. What's more, the kiosk is a controlled environment. It presents the image that you want to communicate and allows you to determine the type and level of information your customers can access. A good interactive kiosk should be designed to be user friendly, attracting both the Internet/PC literate customer and people who would not normally use a computer. Kiosks offer *broad reach* across different market sectors and customer groups.

Primary applications for iKiosks in e-business and e-marketing

1. **Acquisition.** Whether you need to target customers in a public access area, or at a communal point within a company, the kiosk makes an excellent, interactive information point. At locations such as exhibitions and seminars, for example, kiosks can deal with a huge range of routine enquiries and capture data on passing customers who may not wish to talk to a salesperson. This enables your staff more time to handle complex issues and provide personal service to customers who need it.

2. **Communications.** In the workplace, interactive kiosks can be used for corporate communications, giving everyone the opportunity to keep up with company news. When used in conjunction with a card reader and PIN code, it can provide selective access to company reports and databases, as well as shopping, enabling the kiosk to capture information as well as providing it. Kiosks are much more than intelligent information centres. They are also invaluable as multimedia entertainment systems that engage and amuse customers. The kiosk is self-operated and works without human supervision, so it can be available for 24 hours a day. In a busy sales area it reduces customer walkouts by holding attention and by providing information. It can answer sales queries, provide up-to-date prices and confirm delivery times.

3. **Selling.** You can also use interactive kiosks as a window to your e-business. This means that you can take advantage of all the benefits of the Internet and web, within a controlled environment, selling products through the kiosk and capturing customer data. This can include taking credit card orders or allowing B2B clients to place orders on account.

1.3 e-Business demographics

Who accesses the web?

Globally, it is estimated that over 400 million people have access to the Internet and web. By far the largest online population is in the USA and Canada, with over 167 million people using the Internet. In Europe, 113.4 million people are online, of which the UK contributes around 19 million, representing 40%

of the total UK population. This demonstrates significant growth over 1998, when only 25% of UK adults had access, and 7% in 1997. The art of estimating how many people are online is an incredible difficult one as the numbers are constantly changing. However, by pulling together data from a variety of sources, NUA Internet Surveys has been able to come up with these figures:

Table 1.1   Global Internet access – Nua Internet Surveys, April 2001. Note that the figures shown are for November 2000.

World Total	407.1 million
Africa	3.1 million
Asia/Pacific	104.9 million
Europe	113.4 million
Middle East	2.4 million
Canada & USA	167.1 million
South America	16.5 million

The majority of UK web access comes from two core age brackets. 70% are 18 – 24 year-olds, who are typically accessing the web for entertainment, whilst 82% of 35 – 54 year-olds log on for news and information. However, there are two important user groups of the Internet and web developing, both demonstrating strong characteristics to buy online. The first, and possibly one of the most important and potentially influential markets to emerge is the youth sector, representing a community of Internet-savvy individuals with a high degree of disposable income and a passion for branded goods, music and fashion accessories. The second is women. Currently, research shows that 44% of the UK Internet audience are women, representing yet another extremely powerful market opportunity.

One of the biggest issues that continues to face the online space and slowed the pace of e-business development in the UK, has been the penetration of modems to computers, both in the workplace and the home. Today, when you buy a PC, it comes already 'Internet-enabled', providing a built-in modem and all the software you need to access the Internet, including software from an ISP (Internet Service Provider) and a free Internet browser. Surveys, conducted across the country, have revealed that around 35% of UK web users access the Internet from home, whilst the business sector remains slow to offer access to employees from their own desktops. This is typically out of fear of abuse; concerns over cost or being able to control how much work time is used productively online.

The fact is the Internet and web have evolved to become an intrinsic part of our daily lives, both at work and at home – for business, pleasure or entertainment.

Future forecast – the Internet tomorrow

The world's GDP is currently around US$30 trillion, of which Europe and North America generate roughly a third each. By 2004, the global business-to-business 'Internet Protocol-based' e-business marketplace is expected to exceed $7 trillion, of which North America's share will approach $2.8 trillion (about 40%) and Europe's will be $2.3 trillion (about 33%), representing some 23% of the European Union's total GDP. Of this e-business, digital trading communities, or e-marketplaces, will account for 56% of trade, according to Forrester Research. There are some 400m people online worldwide today. This figure is expected to rise to over half a billion, or 8% of the world's adult population by 2002. The top 15 countries account for nearly 82% of these worldwide Internet users, and seven of the top 15 will be European by the end of 2001. Online retail sales in Europe are predicted to almost double annually over the next five years, from 2.9 billion euros in 1999 to 175 billion euros in 2005, representing 7% of Europe's retail sales. Approximately two-thirds of German, French and UK net users visit e-retail sites and, like US Internet users, almost half of them can be expected to purchase products or services online. PCs will remain the overwhelming Internet access device for now, and the number of e-mail accounts worldwide grew by 83% in 1999 to 569m accounts, a rate that, if it continues, as expected, will lift the tally past telephone lines or television sets within just a few years. But more people will use television sets to go online than PCs by 2005, and by 2006, information appliances will match the number of PCs used for web access. Eighty million European households will be using interactive TV to go online by 2005.

Looking forward to 2010, when 3 billion of the world's population of 10 billion are online and the combined online populations of Europe and the

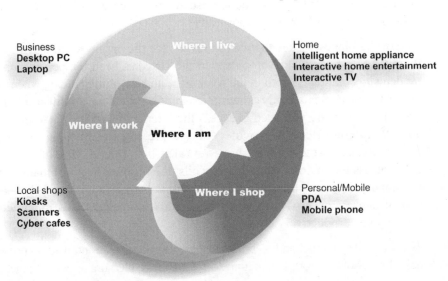

Figure 1.9   Location will have an impact on the way customers access e-businesses

USA comprise less than a sixth of the total online population, the e-world will look very different. The future for e-business looks bright. By 2003, experts at Forrester Research predict that global e-business will represent around 5% of GDP for that year, or $3.2 trillion. In Europe, the statistics are equally impressive. In 1997, European Internet transactions were recorded as being worth $35.8 million. By 2004, e-business is expected to grow to $8 billion.

At present, the trend for e-business has been orientated to business-to-consumer selling, with the sex industry, online books and music stores leading the way. However, the primary application for e-business in the future will be business-to-business, as organizations around the world begin to develop and implement cost-saving strategies for transacting with business partners, suppliers and customers.

USEFUL WEB SITES Referenced in this chapter

Zagme	www.zagme.com
Mviva	www.mviva.com
eMarketer	www.emarketer.com
NUA Internet Surveys	www.nua.ie
Boltblue	www.blood.org
Go Airways	www.go-fly.com
British Airways	www.britishairways.com
Forrester Research	www.forrester.com

CHAPTER SUMMARY

In this chapter, you have learnt:

1. That e-business is the process of moving internal and external processes to the Internet.

2. That new media channels go beyond the Internet. They encompass mobile devices, digital TV and Interactive Kiosks.

3. That the customer sits at the centre of e-business and wants to access your organization through all or any one of the multiple touch points available.

4. That mobile devices are becoming an important element of the overall e-marketing and e-business mix.

5. That Internet penetration and adoption rates are increasing year on year.

6. That 'location' is becoming a key driver in the delivery of e-business to your customers.

TEST YOURSELF

1. e-business was largely pioneered by non-traditional bricks and mortar brands such as Amazon and Dell. *True or false?*

2. Short Messaging Service is a mobile phone technology that enables marketers to deliver highly interactive messages to customers, including movies, audio clips and animations. *True or false?*

3. Wireless Application Protocol (WAP) enables web-browsing via your mobile phone handset or Personal Digital Assistant (PDA). *True or false?*

4. GPRS will offer mobile device users a permanent, 'always-on' connection to the Internet using high-bandwidth modems within the mobile devices for interactive content delivery. *True or false?*

5. To use Interactive TV features, your content will need to be redeveloped for that platform. *True or false?*

6. Thanks to Interactive kiosks, the Internet is now available on the high street and in other public places where information is accessible on facilities, products and services available locally. *True or false?*

7. It is estimated that there are currently 407 million people using the Internet worldwide. *True or false?*

8. Research suggests that location will become a major factor influencing the way customers access e-businesses in the future. *True or false?*

9. By 2010, there will be over 50 billion Internet users and e-business revenues will soar to over 50% of the world's GDP for that year. *True or false?*

For the answers to these questions in this book and for further reading on e-business, visit the companion web site at:

www.bh.com/companions/0750652934

Chapter **2**

**Developing the
e-business plan**

OVERVIEW

This chapter introduces the process of e-business planning. It seeks to remove the myths of e-business and help you prepare your case, through tools such as SWOT analysis, cost/benefit analysis, ROI scenarios and winning management support.

LEARNING OBJECTIVES

In this second chapter you will learn:

● How to conduct an e-business SWOT analysis

● How to determine your e-business strategy: Positioning; Product; Pricing and Promotion

● About the importance of identifying the cost – benefit model for e-business

● How to overcome obstacles and gain management 'buy-in' to e-business

Chapter Topic	Specific Learning Objective
2.0 Introduction	How to understand your business and the top ten e-business myths
2.1 e-Business SWOT analysis	How to evaluate your business and see if it's ready for e-business
2.2 Determining your strategy	The planning process and the characteristics of B2B and B2C
2.3 e-Business cost / benefit	Understand how to evaluate different ROI scenarios
2.4 Management buy-in	Developing the compelling business case

KEYWORDS:

SWOT	Stickiness	B2B	B2C	Value chain
Taxation	Management buy-in			

Notepad exercises: 1

2.0 Developing your e-business plan

Developing your e-business plan requires you to make a series of strategic choices and decisions. It will start with a current situation analysis that will identify where you are now and will involve you asking yourself a number of difficult questions about how you manage your business's Internet presence:

1. Do we project a unified web presence, designed to meet the specific needs of our key customers, suppliers or shareholders?

2. Are we organized for effective e-business?

3. Do we encourage creativity, innovation and risk?

4. Do we have established, clear policies on acceptable use, privacy and Internet security?

5. Is our business environment flexible enough to encompass e-business?

6. Are we investing in the appropriate areas to sustain high-level business performance over the long term?

The road to e-business success has been left recently littered with organizations that thought they had done enough in planning their strategy. IBM, one of the world's largest players in e-business, recently published their top ten e-business myths. You may see some that sound strangely familiar to you:

1. With a targeted e-business strategy and a number of initiatives underway, we're on the road to e-business success.

2. A centralized structure is the only way to effectively organize and manage an e-business.

3. Taking the time to develop a formal e-business management system will prevent us from moving at 'e-speed'.

4. An e-business investment should be funded and measured just like any other investment.

5. Our corporate communications policies are well documented - widespread Web publishing poses no real risk.

6. With the right latitude and enough money, an 'e-culture' will emerge.

7. e-Business? Leave it to our techies...

8. Business units, brands and functional groups should be given complete freedom to express themselves.

9. We can just mimic the 'best practices' of another leading e-business.

10. Our e-business transformation is complete.

These are all statements that during your voyage into e-business you will be tempted to say.

2.1 Current situation – the e-business SWOT analysis

By conducting a SWOT analysis, specific to your own organization, you can set the scene for planning and developing the e-business strategy. The analysis will help you determine where your organization sits relative to the internal and external factors that will affect the plan's introduction.

Tip: Your e-business SWOT should consider both the internal factors, such as your systems, management and resources, together with the external factors such as competitors, customers and socio-economics.

NOTEPAD EXERCISE

Using the table below, conduct an e-business SWOT analysis on your own organization. Identify where your organization's key strengths are; where possible weaknesses in your strategy could exist; what online opportunities exist to take advantage of and where potential threats will come from.

So how does the e-business SWOT work?

Below is an example of an e-business SWOT analysis.

STRENGTHS

- Flexibility and adaptability to market movement
- Brand strength and positioning
- Management commitment to e-business
- Customer willingness to adopt new channels
- Effective delivery processes – can deliver, anytime, anywhere

WEAKNESSES

- Inflexibility to respond to e-business opportunity due to legacy systems
- Weak brand – not associated with Internet trading
- Weak leadership – lack of commitment from management to buy-in to e-business
- No strategy – lack of planning to implement e-business activity
- No ability to fulfil – global channels offer global customers

OPPORTUNITIES

- Access to new customers and markets

- Ability to deliver new products and services – differentiated from traditional business

- New channel of distribution

- Improvements in operational efficiency

THREATS

- Known competitors moving into your territory – customers may switch

- New products – customers may demand a different product online

- Speed of response – legacy may prohibit our ability to move fast enough

- Channel conflicts – offline channels may resist e-business model

- Customer choice – more choice, access and price flexibility/ transparency

- Regulation – legislation changes and differences at local levels

2.2 Determining your e-business strategy

Many e-businesses measure their success by the number of hits (visits) they get, not the number of customers they attract or sales they make. Unfortunately, this gives an unrealistic view of how well, or badly, the site is doing. True success depends upon your overall e-business strategy.

Understanding the differences between B2B and B2C e-business

The Internet offers new opportunities for both traditional bricks-and-mortar and emerging 'dotcom' businesses to extend their business reach while integrating their business processes at the same time.

e-Business opportunities fall into three distinct groups:

1. Business-to-Consumer (B2C)

2. Business-to-Business (B2B)

3. Business-to-Enterprise (B2E)

B2C applications often deal with extending the reach of the organization to their consumer market via the Internet. Historically, much of the B2C e-business conducted and publicised has involved disparate web applications that are not integrated into the business, but exist separately. B2C transactions online are typically referred to as eCommerce and involve credit or debit card payments.

B2B applications employ Internet technologies that link one organization with another, many of whom are traditional bricks-and-mortar companies that have been doing business together for a time, using direct connection technologies to trade with each other, such as Electronic Data Interchange (EDI).

B2E however, typically involves 'internal' business processes that can be moved to the Internet specifically for the benefit of an organization's staff, such as messaging using mobile devices, stock look-ups from remote locations using PDAs or Intranet facilities.

Recently, much of the e-business we hear about concerns B2C e-commerce, principally because the consumer brands were early adopters of selling online their 'mass-market' products. These operations utilized highly attractive, graphical-designed web sites to capture consumer interest. B2C web businesses have also integrated 'stickiness', to encourage users to buy and return to conduct repeat transactions.

Tip: Stickiness relates to a web site's ability to retain users for lengthy periods of time, through interactive or useful content and tools.

Additionally, consumer-led e-business has been highly publicized due to dot.com startups receiving large amounts of venture capital, such as boo.com – a brand we discuss in Chapter 11. However, research studies suggest that the B2B segment will prove to be much more significant in terms of overall e-business economic impact, perhaps by an order of magnitude. Companies that succeed in building effective B2B capabilities are likely to experience:

- Increased customer loyalty
- Reduced operational costs
- Reduced customer costs
- Improvements in service
- Increases in revenue

If you compare B2C e-business with B2B, you will notice that they are very different in their requirements. The following table demonstrates this.

Table 2.1   B2B Vs B2C Characteristics

Characteristic	B2B	B2C
Strategy	High	Medium
Creativity and branding	Low	High
Technology	High	Medium
Value-chain Integration	High	Medium – Low
Legacy system Integration	High	Low

As the chart demonstrates, in B2C the offering is conceived from back to front – meaning that the business is more orientated towards building a front-end, web-based business than building a back-end web-based business, as appropriate to B2B. The B2C proposition is further differentiated from B2B in the way that B2C generates income. Typically, a consumer-led transactional site will involve various presentation technologies, such as Flash, and utilize eCommerce engines, such as shopping baskets, linked to simple legacy systems such as basic stock information at the bricks-and-mortar end.

CASE STUDY: FILOFAX UK

A good example of a non-integrated e-business in the B2C sector is Filofax, the manufacturers and global retailers of personal organizer products. Filofax now sells large volumes of its personal organizer products online. Their web site is very effective, easy to use and graphically pleasing, but sits separately from their organization in terms of finance, manufacturing, purchasing and fulfilment to the customer.

Figure 2.1   The Filofax web site

The key business objective for B2C sites is to generate income through online sales of products or via advertising revenue. Very little, if any, of the B2C focus is attached to leveraging the entire business value chain for cost efficiencies, improved service and customer lock-in that can be achieved. In contrast, B2B e-business focuses on leveraging the value chain to provide better service and support to its business customers. In doing so, B2B sites create barriers to entry, including 'switching costs' that prevent customers from making easy transitions to alternative suppliers. Unlike the B2C sector, B2B e-businesses tend to be highly complicated in a variety of ways. First, B2B focus on designing the site with the business customer's online experience in mind. The site will focus less on advertising banners, flashy graphics, and other 'creative' experiences and more on providing information in the easiest, fastest and most navigable manner. B2B sites also integrate the end-customer's way of trading, to include integrating their existing buyer profiles, preferences, contractual arrangements, preferred payment methods and their information needs. This means that the B2B e-business will have invested heavily in complex integration – not only with legacy systems and architectures, but also with the systems of customers, partners, and suppliers as well. For the B2B organization, e-business means it's more about back-end functionality, rather than flashy front ends.

In summary, the benefits of B2B e-business are about more than market share – they are about developing dramatic business impacts that improve efficiency, customer-loyalty and profitability. Benefits include:

- Effective and more profitable customer service
- Streamlining business processes
- Integration of value chain
- Integration of customers through relationship redefinition.

Understanding the online buying cycle

Understanding your customers and how they buy online will be a key stage in developing your e-business strategy, from the customer perspective.

There are, in essence, eight stages, each of which when analyzed allows us to break down our e-business strategy into manageable chunks that we can plan.

1. Know your customer

The first step in knowing your customer is to identify and define who are your online customers. They may not be the same as your traditional offline customers. For example, they may exist in other geographic territories that you have not traded with before. *First*, ask yourself these questions:

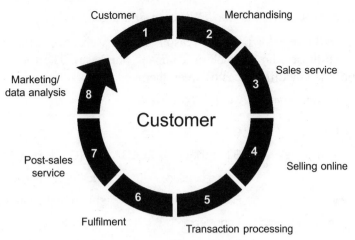

Figure 2.2   The online buying cycle – from the customer perspective

- Who are my largest customer groups?
- Where are they?
- Are they decision makers or researchers?
- Are they loyal to my brand?

Second, decide what they want to buy from you. Ask yourself:

- Will the products we currently sell through traditional channels migrate well to the web, or are they too complex, cumbersome and difficult to communicate online?

Third, think about how often they are likely to purchase. Ask yourself:

- Are my customers frequent purchasers, annual purchasers or will they buy ad-hoc?

And *last*, how much help will you need to provide in their purchasing decision making process?

If you are B2B, you may wish to ask yourself these questions of your customers:

- What type of business are they? (Use Industry SIC codes.)
- What size of business are they?
- How many locations do they have?
- How many employees do they have that will want to buy from our site?
- What decision-making process do they have?
- What customer data do we have? (Frequency; Recency; Value; Usage rate)

Once you have the answers to these questions, you can move on with the plan.

The differences between B2B and B2C customers online

Consumers buying for personal reasons on the web have different buying habits than those who are making company purchases. The following chart identifies the key differences between them.

Table 2.2   The differences between B2B and B2C customers

Characteristic	B2B	B2C
Market size and value	$1.3 trillion by 2003	$110 billion by 2003
	Cross-border	Not cross-border
Customer volumes	Fragmented	1-to-many individuals
Relationship requirements	Long-term	Short-term
	Mission-critical	Transactional
	High-switching costs	Low-switching costs
Product attributes	Customized	Mass market
Complex	Large purchase size	Small purchase size
Stickiness	High	Low
	Stay with one site	Multi-site purchasing
Buying process	Planned and formal	Spontaneous
	Negotiated pricing	Not negotiated
	PO/account payment	Credit card payment

2. Products and Services

Once you have determined who your customers are and what they want to buy from you, the next stage in developing your e-business plan is to determine which products and/or services you will offer. This process should include determining pricing and how you are going to deliver.

3. Sales Support

Dealing with a customer's question and/or problem before and after the sale online is extremely complex. We tackle this issue head on in Chapter 6, but for your e-business, you will need to develop processes to handle inbound and outbound voice and e-mail traffic generated by your site, as well as mechanisms for tracking complaints, escalating them and ensuring they are resolved within the timescale you have quoted.

4. Selling Online

For the e-business, the question of selling online is an easy one to answer – Yes! Of course we want to sell online and generate income from that activity.

But how? To be able to sell online, you will need some kind of eCommerce engine integrated into your site, such as shopping basket and credit card payment processing system for the B2C brand, or if you are a B2B brand, integration with your offline accounting systems.

5. Transaction Processing

This step will see you determining how will you handle:

- Orders received via the site?
- Taxation? Particularly for overseas orders.

Accepting online payments

Most customers will expect to pay for goods and services ordered online by credit or charge card. To facilitate this, your e-business plan will need to include the creation of a merchant account with your bank. If you already have merchant status, you will need to receive authorization from your bank to accept credit and debit card transactions over the Internet.

Payment processing

You can receive customer credit card details via secure forms on your web site and process them instantly through an online payment gateway. Online processing involves secure, real-time, online credit and debit card transaction, authorization and clearance. The security and privacy of all card details are maintained and transactions can be authorized within seconds. All transactions are then cleared through your acquiring bank at the end of the day.

Online credit card processing follows three steps

Authentication: ensure that the card(s) have authentic numbers, have actually been issued and have not been reported stolen.

Authorization: check whether the funds are available for purchase. If they are the funds are reserved, but the actual money is not transferred as yet.

Settlement: once the products are shipped to the customer then you let the banks know. The banks then release the reserved funds, and the money makes its way through various intermediaries to your account.

Order processing

To process orders effectively, you must consider each stage of the process.

Table 2.3   e-Business order processing

Inventory	Are you only willing to supply items in stock or can you afford to order items from a supplier?
Out of Stock	When should you inform customers if an item is out of stock or likely to take extra delivery time?

Back Orders	When should you notify visitors of a back order? When they're checking out? After they've placed an order? Or would you prefer to recommend an alternative solution?
Controls	If your inventory is at a minimum, will you put up a barrier to say products can't be offered? Will this policy apply to all products or be different for different products?
Partial Sales	What will you do if part of an order is returned to you?

6. Fulfilment

Are you able to manage customer expectations?

What type of delivery service will you be able to offer?

7. After-sales Services

Will you offer additional customer support?

Will you provide an online order/shipping status feature?

8. Performance Analysis

What kind of information do you want to capture?

How will you use it to improve your business?

Alternatively, for corporate customers you can offer them an online account. This enables them to purchase via your site without the need to enter their credit card details.

Other issues to consider in planning for e-business

Taxation in e-business

As you'd expect this is a minefield. Tax policies not only differ between countries, in America they differ between states. Consult a taxation expert or invest in a locally built back-end system that automatically calculates tax on your behalf.

Terms and conditions

It is essential to have a list of 'Terms and Conditions' on your site. It should be displayed on your site and easily accessible for viewing by customers, *before* they commit to a purchase. In most cases, customers will buy from an e-business that offers them a secure and reliable service. Managing customer expectations is vital if you don't want to disappoint them. There are various issues related to delivery such as timing, updating of orders and customer service that play a vital part in making sure your first customers become loyal customers.

Payment

Whatever you do, don't charge customer's credit cards until the products are shipped or delivered. In the mail-order business, technically the merchant (you) is not allowed to move money immediately unless the product is delivered or shipped *on the same day*.

Manage customer expectation

Due to the dynamic nature of e-business, customer expectations of online ordering are heighten. Managing customer expectation is vital if you don't want to disappoint them. For instance, never promise next day delivery unless you are sure you can deliver and your customers are willing to pay the price.

Delivery charges

It's important to remember that the cost of sending out a product isn't necessarily what you will charge to the customer. The actual cost should instead be what it costs you to deliver a convenient customer service. You should devote a page of your site to explaining how your delivery charges are structured and give customers the choice to choose their preferred method of delivery. There is nothing worse for a customer to go through the whole ordering process only to see a shocking delivery charge added to the cost of the goods.

International delivery

If you decide to offer international delivery, you may want to use different carriers for various delivery zones.

Timing

If customers order late in the day, what are the chances you'll be able to reach the post in time? Talk to your courier before you decide on a cut-off time. Then make sure you ask your customers exactly when they want their product delivered, and charge accordingly.

Customer service

When problems arise, customers will telephone you to find out what's going on. Ensure you have the mechanisms, capacity and resources in place to handle inbound calls and e-mails, so that you can answer queries within a sensible timescale.

Updating orders

Should your fulfilment centre inform the system when an order has been shipped? Is there a shipping number to be attached to an order number? Does shipping status require updating, and if so how often?

Order status

Should you provide customers with a facility to look up their shipping status on-line? If there are any changes to the customer order, should they be emailed in advance? When you accept their order will you send confirmation?

Technical support

Will you offer additional customer support with your products e.g. self-assembly radios, and if so does it need to be processed as an additional order?

Local support

If you're operating at a global level, you will need to consider languages, currencies and regional pricing structures.

Security

Because the Internet is a public network, anyone can access it, which is why some customers can be nervous about giving their credit card details over the Net. However, there are several ways around this:

- Most modern browsers now have security built-in so that unauthorized persons cannot read, forge or intercept an on-line transaction.

- If you're with an ISP, ask if they host secure transactions, supported by encryption standards like SSL (Secure Sockets Layer) and SET (Secure Electronic Transaction).

- If you publish information, your customers are likely to visit your site several times. Set up password-controlled subscriptions to your site.

- If your customers are still nervous, you can take most of their order on your web site, then call them back for their credit card details, or allow them to pay by post.

Encrypting orders

Encryption technology scrambles a message so that only the intended recipient can unscramble it. To implement this kind of technology you or your ISP will need to enable SSL on your web server. But please bear in mind that it will only work with other SSL-friendly servers. Today, most servers do support SSL, but you need to consider whether they're the ones your visitors will be using.

Enrich the site

Because many people are wary of shopping on-line I recommend you include a section on your web site outlining the measures you've taken to address the problem. It should include the following:

Table 2.4 – Building Customer Confidence in e-business

Highlight any security measures	You have in place e.g. encryption, firewall protection.
Feature secure site symbols	A complete key on Explorer, a locked padlock on Navigator.
Highlight a good track record	If you have had no problems with security, say so.
Consider offering a guarantee	This will give consumers more confidence.
Contact consumer organizations	Such as Which? who if you meet with their security standards, will allow you to use their logos.

Legal issues

Naturally we can't attempt to cover all the legal angles in this book, but before you consult a legal professional I recommend you consider these questions:

- What policies and disclaimers must be made available to customers?

- What are your Terms and Conditions of Sale?

- What is your Returns Policy?

- Do you offer Guarantees or Limited Warranties?

- Are there any locations where a retailer cannot legally sell your products?

If your lawyer doesn't understand e-business, you may wish to find one that does.

2.3 The e-business cost/benefit analysis

Earlier in the chapter, we looked at some of the benefits of e-business: to recap, these included loyalty; profitability; value chain integration and relationship management. But if you are to win the support for eBusiness of your executive, how do justify the cost?

Now I'm no cost/benefit analyst, so I'll only tackle the subject in brief, but identifying the e-business cost/benefit requires the use of cost/benefit analysis tools. This process is widely used, not just online but offline, to support eBusiness planning, decision-making, performance evaluation and other purposes that may be specific to your organization. Cost / Benefit analysis requires that you review and weight both the positive and negative impacts of eBusiness to your organization and its customers.

The following are some of the key *costs* you may have to evaluate and weight:

- Hardware
- Software licensing
- Internal human resources
- External resources
- Annual service contracts to maintain your e-business site/solution.

Once again, some of the key *benefits* your organization and its customers may gain from e-business are:

- Increased productivity through enhanced accessibility to the organization, its products, services and information.
- The automation of critical business processes, such as procurement, sales, marketing and CRM, enabling employees and customers to administer corporate services on their own, thus leveraging the self-service nature of e-business.
- Reduced costs of distribution, including technical, sales and marketing and customer information, all lowering corporate communications costs.
- Increased effectiveness at generating revenue, through servicing many customers simultaneously.

Self-service – giving customers and partners the ability to manage their relationship with your organization, via the web browser

A good cost/benefit analysis for e-business will include a time dimension. In order to evaluate the cost / benefit analysis properly, you will need to understand the timing of expected incomings and outgoings and chart these over a defined period, such as 1, 3 or 5 years.

A good cost/benefit analysis will also attempt to quantify every possible benefit and cost that your e-business plan will have, for inclusion in your financial analysis, even intangible or 'soft' costs and benefits, such as brand and customer goodwill. It is important to quantify everything possible as if you don't place a value against every agreed cost or benefit, it contributes nothing to the financial analysis, thereby making it impossible to weight its importance.

For example, if part of your eBusiness investment involves developing your brand, to improve the organization's professional image in the online space, how much monetary value should be credited to this benefit? It will be valued at zero if an acceptable valuation cannot be agreed.

So, in summary, cost/benefit analyses are undertaken to support decision-making processes in relation to your e-business plan. The objective is always to understand the net effect of a decision on the plan and how much that decision will effect revenue, profitability and overall e-business performance.

To support your e-business cost/benefit analysis, we have devised a spreadsheet that you can download and use from the e-business companion web site at: www.bh.com/companions/0750652934.

2.4 Getting management buy-in

Getting management to buy into e-business will require the development of a compelling business case for e-business investment.

Every e-business project has to have a compelling business case. Making the case is difficult but has to be done well. Done badly, not only will there be no funds but, perhaps more critically, senior management will not appreciate and support the necessary changes in organization, culture, processes and business practices. Done well, the case demonstrates and builds support for the changes needed for e-business initiatives to succeed.

Making a compelling business case requires you to:

- Demonstrate why e-business is a strategic must for the organization;
- Quantify the benefits of e-business to the organization, at a detailed level;
- Be specific about how e-business will achieve those benefits.

Therefore, getting management buy-in for e-business can be broken down into the following chunks:

1. Start at the beginning

Define what is e-business is and how it will help the organization achieve its business goals. Confusingly, there are now more flavours of e-business than there Ben & Jerry's ice creams. Be specific about your approach to e-business and explain how it fits within the context of the organization, its markets, customers and partners.

2. Think about e-business applications

What can e-business offer the organization and its various stakeholders in the value chain, that other traditional business processes can't? Take a close look at some of the many e-business approaches being implemented and summarize the Strengths, Weaknesses, Opportunities and Threats of implementing e-business. (Refer back to the e-business SWOT analysis on Page 26).

3. Calculate the costs

Introducing e-business will require a substantial budget. Propose a budget for the project, including costs for technology, marketing, human resources, cultural changes, etc.

4. Calculate the benefits

Integrating e-business into your organization offers improvements in operational efficiency, customer retention, profitability and so on. This is a difficult one to place hard numbers against, but be as specific as you can.

5. Assess the impact and risk

Give the management team an honest assessment of the likely impacts of e-business to the organization and the likely risks that may be encountered along the way.

6. Think about Return On Investment (ROI)

Presenting the ROI scenario(s) for e-business is difficult, but has to be done well. Done badly, not only will there be no funds but, perhaps more critically, senior management will not appreciate and support the necessary changes you are proposing to make in the organization to its culture, processes and business practices. Done well, the e-business ROI demonstrates and builds support for the changes needed. Most ROI calculations are multi-purpose. They satisfy the need to convince, obtain resources and control.

Be prepared to answers questions from senior management along the lines of "Where will e-business add value?" and "If we do this e-business initiative, what's in it for me?"

7. Present your plan

Treat your business case as a board-level presentation by formally presenting it to the entire management team. Show them the 'big picture' and prove to them that e-business will add value throughout all business processes. Convince your management team that they will gain from embracing e-business. Show them:

1. How e-business will support the organization's business strategy and goals.

2. You have identified the best options and explored all alternatives.

3. The 'real' costs and benefits. e-Business will change the nature of the organization and that is likely to affect associated cash flows.

4. The impact and risks associated to e-business, such as financial, market, operational and technical.

5. How e-business will maximize resources and assets. These resources and assets can include cash, sales and marketing time, customers, market share or economies of scale.

Convince managers that they will gain: answer the 'What's in it for me?' syndrome.

Show the personal benefits to the decision makers of backing the e-business initiative. For example, some managers embrace high risk, high reward projects (young, ambitious, reasonable exit from the business or nearing retirement wanting to make their mark) whilst others are more cautious. Others are motivated by leadership and innovation – being the first; by challenges or by large profits or bonuses.

Overall, treat the presentation as a 'sell'!

8. Prove e-business will add value

- Is e-business worthwhile – will it increase profits?
- Will e-business increase shareholder and stakeholder value?
- Is e-business the best investment to make over and above other alternatives?

USEFUL WEB SITES **Referenced in this chapter**

Filofax UK   www.filofax.co.uk

CHAPTER SUMMARY

In this chapter, you have learnt:

1. That a critical analysis and evaluation of your organization and capability is critical to planning e-business.

2. That by conducting an e-business SWOT analysis of Strengths, Weaknesses, Opportunities and Threats, you can identify internal and external factors that will help or hinder you in delivering e-business to your customers.

3. That the characteristics of e-business are different for B2B and B2C markets, where B2B e-business concentrates on operational efficiency and process improvement, whilst B2C focuses on income generation through product/service sales and advertising.

4. That the online buying cycle comprises of 8 key stages: acquisition; merchandising; self-service; selling; transaction processing; fulfilment; post-sales support and data analysis (retention and CRM).

5. That getting management buy-in for e-business requires a thorough understanding of all aspects of the organization and the benefits e-business offers it.

TEST YOURSELF

1. An e-business investment should be funded and measured just like any other investment when developing an e-business strategy. *True or false?*

2. Hits are a useful measure of e-business success. *True or false?*

3. B2B e-business customers demonstrate the same characteristics as B2C e-business customers. *True or false?*

4. Stickiness is a method of ensuring that your e-business site retains visitors for longer and that they return more frequently. *True or false?*

5. B2B brands can benefit from reduced costs, enhanced customer loyalty, greater profitability and improved service levels by using e-business. *True or false?*

Chapter **3**

The online
buying process

OVERVIEW

This chapter describes the online buying process, its similarities with and differences from the traditional buying model, and considers the reasons why you should develop an e-business strategy. We will also look at one of the key challenges faced by e-businesses – price transparency – and review one of the emerging e-business models, the e-marketplace.

LEARNING OBJECTIVES

In this chapter you will learn about:

- The online buying process and how it differs from traditional buying models
- How e-business will affect *your* sales proposition
- The impact of transparent pricing online
- The benefits e-business offers *you* and *your* customers
- The emergence of e-marketplaces
- The changes e-business brings to the customer relationship
- Integrating e-business with *your* Customer Relationship Management (CRM) strategy

Chapter Topic	Specific Learning Objective
3.1 The online buying process	Understand the key stages of the online trading cycle
3.2 Price transparency	3 ways to overcome price transparency
3.3 The benefits	To understand the business and customer benefits of e-business
3.4 e-Marketplaces	To understand the role of e-marketplaces and the benefits of e-procurement
3.5 e-Business and traditional channels	To understand how to integrate e-business with the offline channels

KEYWORDS

| Up-sell | Cross-sell | Price Transparency | e-Procurement e- |
| Marketplace | Acquisition | CRM | Freedom of movement |

Notepad exercises: 1

3.0 Introduction

In many respects, buying and selling on the Internet is little or no different from buying and selling using other traditional channels. So, if this is the case, why do online brands make life so difficult for themselves and their customers to transact over the Internet? Let's analyse the traditional offline buying process and overlay this with the online buying process, in an attempt to identify the similarities and differences, and try to understand how to develop an e-business proposition that makes buying easy for the buyer and selling easy for the seller – 'best practice e-business'. Additionally, for every business activity, there has to be a reason for doing it. A business case that states 'if we do this, then that will happen'. The same applies to e-business and any form of new media marketing, regardless of which channel we are using.

In this chapter, we will also consider the reasons for developing an e-business strategy and what benefits *you* can expect to achieve and pass on to *your* customers.

NOTEPAD EXERCISE

Jot down as many business and customer benefits to e-business as you can think of appropriate to your own organization and markets.

3.1 The online buying process

The objective of any e-business-based business is to develop an ongoing relationship with its customer that results in improved loyalty, repeat purchases and enhanced profitability.

To achieve this, the online business must develop its e-business strategy to encompass a number of different processes. Here are seven:

1. Customer acquisition.

The first process is promotion of the site to the target market(s), which we will discuss in much greater detail later in the book. With volumes of visitors hitting the desired target, the site must encourage users to browse the online 'shop' and provide some information about them-selves through an online registration process. This is the user acquisition stage.

The cost of acquisition is substantially less online that it is offline. It is estimated, that acquiring new customers via a truly customer-centric e-business site accounts for approximately 2% of the cost of acquiring the same customer through traditional offline channels.

2. Segmentation and targeting.

The next step is the collation of user profiles, enabling some segmentation and targeting of customers to take place by type, geographic location, product interest and so on. The objective is to be able to identify customers as individuals, rather than one homogenous market group that all share the same characteristics.

3. Promotions

With user profiling beginning to identify and build individual needs and wants, the e-business can then begin to specifically promote and offer relevant products and services, based on what it knows customers want, rather than assumes. This begins the process of personalization and true 'relationship commerce', which we will discuss later in Chapter 9.

4. Online ordering

Having offered customers the products or services they want, the site must then be able to fulfil a customer's desire to purchase by facilitating easy online ordering. This involves making the selection of products quick and easy. For B2C customers, this will probably be facilitated by way of a shopping basket and incorporating secure credit card transaction processing to complete the sale. In the case of B2B customers, they will require a unique username and password log-in facility that will enable them to gain access to their customer profile, order history, preferential pricing, etc. and to buy 'on account'.

5. and 6. Fulfilment and after-sales support

With the online order process completed, the next major challenge for the e-business is to meet the customer's expectations of fulfilment and be able to offer and deliver after-sales support either via the web site or directly through a call centre or help-desk. The ability to meet delivery and support expectations of any customer, on or offline, will dramatically affect whether or not a customer returns and makes a repeat purchase. The fact is, that with e-business most customer expectations of a supplier are heightened, due to the fact that they are dealing direct and by electronic means.

7. Up-sell and cross-sell

The final process in the online trading lifecycle is being able to encourage customers to come back and buy again. If you can achieve this, then you have the additional opportunity of *cross-selling* and *up-selling* products that you know your customer will be interested in.

Up-sell is to increase a customer's average order value (AOV) through directing them to more expensive products and services, selling them higher numbers of items, or interesting them in longer-term commitments.

Cross-sell is closely related to up-selling. It offers customers access to products or services that they may not have expected. For example, a car manufacturer may sell cars, but it may also provide a branded credit card for owners.

To achieve this, an e-business should mirror online its traditional activities offline. For example, if a customer visits the site to buy a set of skis, it should offer them an incentive to buy new ski boots, the bindings and wax, plus all the other important accessories before they get to the point of purchase and finalize the transaction.

So how does e-business differ to traditional business?

Fundamentally, e-business is little different to traditional business, except we are using different channels and some variations on the rules of engagement to conduct and transact business. The key is to use existing marketing and sales knowledge and experience but apply it online.

In summary, there are three key differences:

1. e-Business offers enhanced speed to market, whereas traditional business can often take months to achieve measurable results.

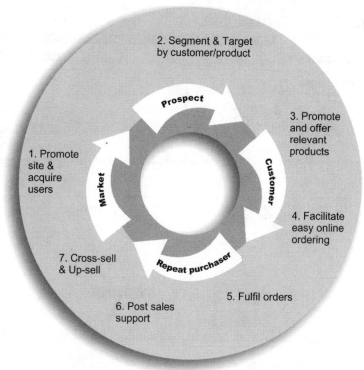

Figure 3.1   The online trading life cycle

2. e-Business is dynamic, enabling purchase decisions to be made and executed in one easy process within hours, whereas traditional forms of commerce can often take days, weeks or months for the transactions to take place.

3. e-Business enables any organization to serve many customers at one time, thereby offering economies of scale and enhanced profitability, whereas traditional channels are bound by operating restrictions such as staff, business hours, geography and so on…

3.2 Price transparency

While representing a new channel to market and an increased opportunity to do business with a greater number of customers, online channels, such as the Internet, also represent a major risk. Online, there is an abundance of free, easily obtainable information that poses a major threat to business. For the first time in business history, the power really has shifted to the customer who can use online channels to see your products and services, review your prices and compare them, at the click of a mouse, with your competition.

Figure 3.2   The home page of price comparison site LetsBuyIt.com

The emergence of sites like www.letsbuyit.com and www.kelkoo.com have shifted the power to the buyer by enabling them to review and rate your prices against everyone else's, in one place – we call this price transparency.

Price transparency creates havoc for the e-business and its online brand. It minimises *your* opportunity to communicate the values of your product and justify your premium prices.

So how do we overcome price transparency?

Addressing transparency in e-business strategy

There are fundamentally three ways to do this:

1. Be innovative in your approach to the online audience and the products/ services you sell.

2. Bundle product offers by adding value to individual products through creating associations with others that enhance the sales proposition.

3. Use creative pricing/new pricing models specific to the channel, to keep you ahead of the competition.

The table below demonstrates the problems with price transparency on the Internet and the ways in which your e-business strategy can overcome it.

Table 3.1   Overcoming price transparency strategy

Issue with price transparency	Strategies to overcome price transparency
Reduces margins	Be innovative: Create new products and services that will enhance customers' lives
Commoditization	Bundle your products and services: Offer customers 'added value' not obtainable elsewhere
Reduces customer brand loyalty	Be creative: Use different pricing models based on the way customers buy from you
Creates poor customer perception	Reward customers for repeat purchasing by enabling them to create an account and only see 'their' specific pricing based on previous purchase history

3.3 e-Business: the benefits

For e-business to be a successful factor in any organization's business process, it has to offer both *your* customer and *your* company a range of benefits not currently available through offline channels. When embarking on an e-business strategy, you must present clear benefits to your customers.

Benefits to your customer

e-Business, when developed properly, can offer customers access to specific and relevant information that meets their needs, not as a consumer group matching a particular demographic profile, but as an individual customer with unique requirements, needs and wants. Another significant benefit of e-business to the end customer is the medium's ability to provide an enhanced level of customer service. As part of an eCRM system, which will be discussed in Chapter 9, service levels can be enhanced through the integration of online customer care policies, Internet-based call centres, accessibility by customers to their own data (via an extranet facility) and improved personalization. Finally, e-business can provide customers with a route to accessing the company 24 hours a day, 365 days a year, through what is in essence, a relatively inexpensive and easy to use medium. No longer do your customers have to wait for your sales lines or call centres to open. With e-business, a customer can interact with you at the time they choose, from the location they choose, using the method they choose.

Benefits to your business

e-Business isn't without its benefits to you. In fact, e-business has shown to deliver so many benefits that some major organizations are scaling down their traditional operations, in favour of the new online model, as demonstrated by Amazon.com and Dell Computers. From the sales and marketing perspective, e-business will enable you to manage your customer relationships more effectively, by moving customers through a seamless process of product identification, selection and purchase. The complete sales interaction process becoming streamlined and a positive experience to the customer. Finally, through e-business, you can help your customers gain access to new products and services at a fraction of the time normally taken, reduce their operating costs and streamline their purchasing processes, all of which will lead to an improved and more profitable customer performance and relationship.

3.4 e-Marketplaces and e-procurement

If you are operating in the Business-to-Business space, then enabling your customers to transact with your business through e-procurement solutions will become critical to future survival. As a direct result of the Internet's freedom of information, buyers are now becoming more powerful than sellers, having greater access to more choice, transparent pricing and consolidated purchasing through web sites such as e-marketplaces.

An e-marketplace is a platform for collaboration between buyers and sellers. It unites end-users, wholesalers and suppliers to streamline business procedures, automate procurement, improve productivity and reduce costs.

One such e-marketplace is Covisint. Covisint was founded by members of the automotive industry in the USA to help benefit all participants and transform the industry's business processes. It sets out to create a business community of buyers, sellers, designers, engineers and third parties affiliated with the global automotive industry. Within the Covisint e-marketplace environment, sellers of goods and services will be able to buy goods and services from their own suppliers. Additionally, non-transactional functions such as programme managers and logistics specialists can benefit from a range of tools developed by Covisint that will assist them in fulfilling their roles in areas such as asset utilization, collaborative planning and supply chain management.

THE BENEFITS OF e-MARKETPLACES

For the e-business, there are numerous benefits associated with belonging to an e-marketplace. These include:

1. Significant cost reductions through process integration.

2. Faster channels of communication, reducing order-to-delivery lead times.

3. Cost-effective identification of new suppliers, products and services.

4. Greater price transparency for both buyers and sellers.

5. Increased reach and larger customer bases, plus lower acquisition costs for new customers.

6. Statistical reports on market activity, creating more accurate forecasts and better responsiveness to changing conditions.

7. Elimination of inefficient purchasing procedures.

8. Reduction of anti-competitive practices and industry cartels.

9. Improved staff productivity, by allowing them to concentrate on key relationships outside the marketplace environment.

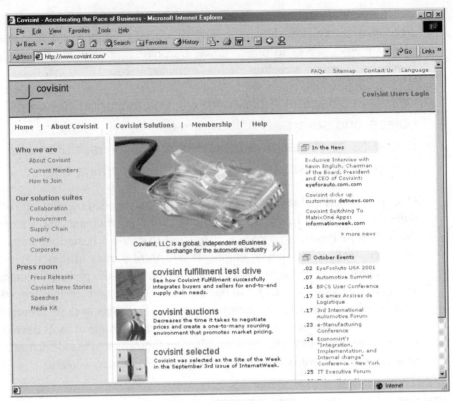

Figure 3.3   Covisint – an e-marketplace for the automotive industry

Recent findings from AMR Research show that nearly 60% of the world's 2,000 largest corporations are already making plans to enter e-marketplaces, and more than half of those that are already involved consider them critical to business success.

Business-to-Business activity is the fastest growing area of e-business. Current forecasts indicate that between 50% and 80% of all Business-to-Business transactions will be conducted through an e-marketplace by the middle of this decade.

The advent of e-procurement has facilitated the need for Business-to-Business (B2B) markets to be developed that streamline selling, procurement and logistics processes and enable buyers and sellers to benefit from a range of cost-saving opportunities.

THE BENEFITS OF e-PROCUREMENT

For the buyer

- Reduced purchasing prices
- Enhanced group purchasing
- Improved budgetary control
- Reduced administrative and paperwork costs
- Reduced buying cycle times
- Improvements in information flow between buyer and seller
- Enhanced relationships resulting in improved contract negotiation
- Improved payment processes

For the seller

- Increased sales
- Enhanced profitability
- Extended market reach
- Reduced sales cycles
- Improved sales productivity
- Streamlined sales processes

For both

- Reduced costs of staffing, administration
- Enhanced customer service levels, specifically technical support
- Reduced product distribution and storage costs, as online procurement facilitates Just-in-Time (JIT) ordering

 ## 3.5 e-Business and the integration of traditional channels

The key to successful e-business is to integrate the traditional buying methods of your customers with the freedom of using online channels when it suits them. The objective is to deliver to customers what I call *'freedom of movement'* (others call 'clicks and mortar' or 'bricks and clicks') – the ability, for example, for a customer to visit your store and select products for purchase, but conduct the buying transaction online from the comfort of their own home later, with the view to you delivering. This is a service that high street book retailer Waterstone's offers. Alternatively, *'freedom of movement'* could involve enabling your customer to have the same 'quality of experience' online as they have offline, by being able to access the same level of information about their relationship with you via the browser, PDA, mobile phone, telephone or physical bricks and mortar environment. Let's look at an example of a business that has integrated its e-business channel with its existing offline channel to offer customers *'freedom of movement'*.

CASE STUDY: LANDS' END

Lands' End, the US-based direct merchant of clothing, home wares and luggage products, was an early adopter of the Internet, launching its web site (http://www.landsend.com) in 1995. Initially, the site featured 100 products as well as stories, essays and travelogues. Today, the US site offers every Lands' End product, including overstocks (excess merchandise) that can be purchased at discounts of up to 75%. In addition, Lands' End have launched web sites in the United Kingdom, Japan, Germany, France, Ireland and Italy.

Figure 3.4   Lands' End Live™, online chat with customer services

During the average year, Lands' End receives around 40,000 to 50,000 customer service calls on a typical day and has more than 1,100 phone lines to handle over 100,000 calls a day at peak times. It also receives around 230,000 e-mails per annum, each of which receives a personal response. However, it was the introduction of **Lands' End Live™** - a feature of their web site that allows customers to talk or 'chat' online directly with their customer service representatives, while shopping at landsend.com – that put them into the 'freedom of movement' category. By clicking on the Lands' End Live button, shoppers can have a direct conversation, 24 hours a day, 365 days a year, with a qualified Customer Services Representative at Lands' End about any of the products or features on landsend.com.

USEFUL WEB SITES Referenced in this chapter

Let's Buy It	www.letsbuyit.com
Kelkoo	www.kelkoo.com
Covisint	www.covisint.com
AMR Research	www.amrresearch.com
Amazon	www.amazon.com
Dell Computers	www.dell.com

CHAPTER SUMMARY

In this chapter, you have learnt that

1. There are seven key stages in the online trading lifecycle: acquisition; segmentation and targeting; promotions; online ordering; fulfilment; support; up-sell and cross-sell.

2. There are three key steps an e-business can take to overcome price transparency: innovate; bundle; create new pricing models.

3. e-Business offers many identifiable benefits to your customers, including access to relevant and timely information, whilst to your business it improves customer management, saves time and reduces overall operational costs.

4. e-Marketplaces and e-procurement can improve operational efficiencies and deliver cost savings in e-business.

5. The integration of your e-business with offline business is key to long-term CRM, as customers require 'freedom of movement' across all trading channels. See Chapter 9 for further reading on eCRM.

TEST YOURSELF

1. The Internet is becoming the transaction channel of choice for business and consumer customers. *True or false?*

2. Selling products and services via the Internet is little different to traditional buying and selling offline. *True or false?*

3. Transparency of pricing online in known to encourage greater customer loyalty. *True or false?*

4. An e-marketplace brings buyers and sellers together to streamline business processes, automate procurement processes and improve productivity / reduce costs. *True or false?*

5. Prospects and customers who use the Web as an information and transaction channel do not tend to use offline channels. Therefore, e-businesses do not need to consider integrating offline businesses with online as part of their long-term CRM strategy. *True or false?*

Chapter 4

e-Branding –
what's in a domain name?

OVERVIEW

This chapter discusses branding. It defines the processes an e-business may go through to develop its online brand and considers some of the risks of moving a traditional brand online, as well as exploring the approach of 'pure-play' Internet brands. In this chapter, we also look at the differences between business-to-business and business-to-consumer brands as well as looking at the challenges a business now faces in registering a domain name.

LEARNING OBJECTIVES

In this fourth chapter you will learn:

- About the importance of developing a tangible online brand identity

- From those who have achieved brand success online and why?

Chapter Topic	Specific Learning Objective
4.0 Introduction	To define and build a Brand
4.1 The tangible e-Brand dilemma	To understand the importance of online branding
4.2 The characteristics of the online brand	To understand what makes an online brand work
4.3 Moving the traditional brand online	To understand the risks of moving your brand online
4.4 The .com strategy	How to approach online brand strategy
4.5 Domain names	How to choose a domain name

KEYWORDS

Brand	Instances of Contact	URL	Domain Name
B2B			

Notepad exercises: 2

4.0 e-Business branding. It's more than a name!

Brand – A product or service augmented in a distinctive way so that customers and users perceive relevant, unique added value matching their needs more closely than competing products or services. Brands are typically protected as a trademark for legal purposes.

A brand is not just a logo or a name. Nor is it just about advertising. In the consumer world, a brand can be defined as a series of messages built around a name, which convey expectations for a distinctive customer experience. For instance, Volvo means 'safety'. In a B2C context, consumers give meaning to a brand in terms of three types of benefits:

1. Product benefits – what is offered (e.g. pricing, product features);

2. Relationship benefits – how it is offered (e.g. the attitudes of direct sales staff);

3. Emotional benefits – what emotions are associated with the brand (e.g. a sense of belonging to a community that uses the brand).

Build your brand and they will come

A recent survey demonstrated the importance of online brand building, as it showed that six out of ten Internet users directly typed into their browser the address of the brand they are interested in buying when looking for a particular product. The results of the ebates.com Dot-Shopper Survey, conducted by Harris Interactive, also showed that banner ads attract the least sophisticated consumers. Furthermore, only 6 percent of potential purchasers are driven to online retailers by offline advertising in other media. The report also showed:

- 5 percent of Internet users are classed as 'E-bivalent Newbies'. This means that they have only recently gained access to the Internet and represent the least interested in e-business.

- 17 percent are 'Time-Sensitive Materialists' who use e-business sites for convenience and to save time.

- 23 percent are in the 'Clicks & Mortar' category. These tend to be female homemakers who research products online, but buy offline as they are worried about privacy and security.

- Young, single, early-adopting, high-earning males are most likely to fall into the 'Hooked, Online & Single' category, which comprises 16 percent of e-business users. This group shop, bank, invest, play games and download software the most often.

- One in 5 users are categorised as 'Hunter-Gatherers'. These are likely to be in their thirties, married with children, and frequent visitors to price comparison sites.

- About the same number are 'Brand Loyalists'. They usually visit sites of known and trusted companies and are the most satisfied with e-business, spending the most online.

So what does this research tell us? Are the starrtups, with their heavy venture capital funding making more success of e-business than traditional brands? Recent evidence has shown that this segment has used substantial funds to generate quick awareness and brand identity through TV, radio and press advertising. The trend for the .com has been to achieve massive exposure by making a loud noise. In this chapter, we will review some of the strategies being employed by .coms and look at why online branding goes well beyond a name. We will also investigate why traditional brands have moved parts of their business to the web, but under the guise of a completely new, unknown name, or those that have well established brand values offline, have gone online with a 'crummy' web offering?

Branding in the online space is not just about awareness. e-branding is a direct result of a series of communications and 'instances of contact' with the company that owns the brand. These communications may include advertising or a call centre talking to the customer, but the e-business brand will also be built on how well and efficiently its web site operates, how reliable it is and, fundamentally, that it delivers to the customer not only what they want to buy at the right price, but a consistently delivered experience, every time.

4.1 The 'tangible e-brand' dilemma

What is the dilemma that traditional and start-up .com brands face? It seems that the expectation of branding for the web is that it must be approached in a completely different way to offline. Not true. For many traditional brands, they have spent decades establishing strong brand values that need to be moved online, in just the same ways as they have been executing them offline. For the pure-play, start-up .com brand, we accept that brand values must be established quickly – this has recently been achieved through a burst of advertising. The start-up .com industry has spent ten of millions of advertising dollars, quite often with poor results as they have chosen such a difficult name to remember.

If there is a dilemma, it is for the start-up that needs to find a brand that:

a) They can register;

b) People will remember;

c) Reflects the business message they wish to communicate.

But what about those traditional brands with decades of heritage that have gone online with completely meaningless brands; unknown names to their existing customers? For example, why, in the financial services sector have established institutions like Prudential and the Co-operative Bank gone online with e-Brands that reflect none of their heritage?

NOTEPAD EXERCISE

Write down five key brand values associated with your organization. Ask yourself, do these values work well online and how does your organization communicate these through the web site.

One could say that the dilemma here is that traditional businesses face an uncertain future in the online world. You could also speculate that they're just not convinced by the web (and other digital media) as potentially profitable channels to market. So, have Prudential, The Co-Op and HFC Bank chosen brands such as Egg and Smile and Marbles because they want to retain an arm's length approach to online business, or because they see having an e-Brand that is more hip and trendy acquiring the right type of customer?

Figure 4.1 Egg's web site Home Page

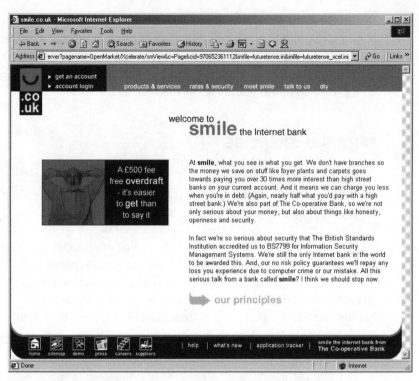

Figure 4.2   Smile's web site Home Page

 ## 4.2 The characteristics of the online brand

Before going online with a brand, it is important to understand what makes the online brand work. Applied Research & Consulting took five hundred and fifty Internet users and divided them up into five age groups and asked them about online brands. The results of this research demonstrated what is important to surfers of all ages. The most important brand characteristics to web users, across the board were:

- Security
- Trustworthiness
- Convenience
- Privacy
- Speed.

Those between 13 and 17 years old, together with those in the 36 to 55 and over age groups stated that in their opinion security was the number one factor, whilst 18 and 25 year olds said convenience was most important to them. In the 26 to 35 years old category, trustworthiness was the primary factor. But what about the B2B e-business brand?

Recently, the web has seen a number of B2B e-businesses, such as Vstream, recently announce the launch of marketing campaigns that you would normally associate with consumer brands, such as amazon.com. VStream, which provides technology for businesses to conduct conference calls and real-time presentations via the Internet, launched a $25m advertising campaign and changed its corporate name to Evoke. But, why is B2B branding important for an e-business? More importantly, what issues does your own business need to consider in order to achieve a successful online B2B brand?

There are several answers to this question. First, a brand is important to B2B companies for the same reasons as for consumer brands. A strong brand defends and differentiates your business from competition helping you to generate sales leads from prospective buyers, command a higher price or suggest your business stands for quality, for example. Second, customers are influenced by a strong B2B brand, as it will help them simplify their purchase decisions and remove some of the noise that the Internet creates by offering so much choice. Third, a brand is important to the B2B e-business as it helps create awareness and goodwill not only amongst its external customers, but internal customers and staff alike.

B2B brands are becoming more critical

The World Wide Web is becoming increasingly more cluttered. This means that the importance of a clearly defined online B2B brand is becoming more critical. Recent studies show that the web now has over 5 million sites and is growing at a rate of approximately 4,500 new sites per day. So what is different with a B2B brand? The main difference between B2C and B2B brands is that consumer brands typically address a single audience made up of individual buyers, whereas, B2B brands often have to deal with a far more complex purchasing model that may comprise multiple touch points in the relationship. The relationship may include corporate purchasers, specifiers and end users.

A good example of a B2B business that has met the challenges of building a successful brand is Intel. For a long time, Intel marketed its products only to engineers and buyers, focusing only on selling the product benefits to targets within their B2B customers. However, Intel quickly recognized that successful B2B branding required them to explore the additional dimension of the end-user market – the consumer. By developing the 'Intel Inside' campaign, Intel managed to generate awareness and demand amongst the PC consumer (end-user) base, which in turn forces PC manufacturers to use Intel chips instead of competing products.

The next challenge for the B2B e-business brand is to ensure that the customer expectation created by the brand are translated into a distinctive customer experience that is consistently delivered. If your business is a service company, this means that your customer-facing staff in sales, call centres and even your web site must consistently deliver the brand promise.

Implications for B2B online branding

Online B2B branding faces the same two challenges as offline branding: the expansion from product benefits to relationship and emotional benefits across all constituents and the consistent delivery of a distinctive customer experience. But these branding challenges in the traditional economy are additionally complex in the B2B e-business world where there needs to be synergy of the offline and online brands.

THREE KEY STEPS to B2B online branding

Online B2B branding is a business-wide issue not just marketing. Achieving a distinctive B2B brand on the Internet requires the e-business to deliver enhanced services and build improved relationships.

Three online initiatives that can facilitate this include:

1. Leveraging the self-service nature of the Internet by providing customer service features such as Client Extranets. Here, you will not only enhance the relationship but achieve customer lock-in at the same time. An important factor in any B2B brands retention strategy.

2. Provide customers with personalization tools, such as personalised environments with tailored content specific to their business. This may include tools, information and pricing that is unique to them.

3. Offer direct methods of communication through a contact strategy that integrates your call centre, account management teams and other customer-facing staff allowing information to be 'pushed' to them instead of solely pulled.

In summary, the development of a successful B2B e-business brand is not solely the remit of marketing, but of the entire business. Successful branding involves the whole company. For your B2B brand to succeed online, you must first address the type of distinctive customer experience you will offer and then adjust your service delivery processes accordingly to meet that. Throughout all aspects of the value chain, branding must be addressed in the same way online as it is in the physical world. Your business must be able to consistently deliver a distinctive, high quality of customer experience, regardless of the channel of delivery.

4.3 Moving the traditional brand online

If you are in a traditional, bricks and mortar organization and planning to develop your brand online as part of the e-business strategy, you must seek to reinforce the corporate offline brand identity within the web site. Companies with well-established offline brands, such as the Ford Motor Company, BMW and Orange, have successfully moved their brands online by displaying the same brand identities within their web sites as they have with TV advertising, direct marketing, shop fronts and so on.

NOTEPAD EXERCISE

Visit the web sites of three well-known traditional brands in your country – the sort you may see frequently on television, the high street or in the press. Can you identify from their web site the same brand values that you have come to recognize them for offline?

But there are associated risks with moving your brand online from a traditional offline position. Customer expectations will be high of the online experience. They will expect to see the same kind of brand performance and equity online as they have been used to seeing offline. However, they could be let down by the e-businesses lack of content, interactivity, ease of use and so on. In many respects, this is one of the reasons we have seen UK brands such as the Co-op Bank and Prudential, move online with brands such as Egg and Smile, (pages 61–62), where they have capitalised on developing new brands that minimise the risk to their existing brands.

 ## 4.4 The .com strategy

Creating an online brand requires an in-depth understanding of your markets and customers. We have already heard how new .com brands that get it wrong can be forgiven by the market, but in the case of established brands the market is far less forgiving. To help you get the e-Branding issue right, here is a well-developed approach to online brand strategy for the e-business.

1. Determine what you are and what you want to say to the online market.

2. Determine how to get your message across.

3. Test market your .com brand for differences in mood and interpretation.

4. Identify your brand values and decide how these will translate online.

5. Test your site using a small group of 'forgiving' customers to check you've got the position and technology right.

6. Research how user-friendly your site is for the target audience.

7. Research your target market and what kinds of sites they look at.

8. Measure the performance of your online brand by evaluating how long customers stay in the site (stickiness) and at what point they exit it.

9. Test your brand regularly to ensure its values are still upheld. Review the parts of the business or process that are letting it down (customer service; fulfilment) and address these quickly.

Table 4.1 *The top 50 online brands, January 2001 according to Cyberatlas*

1	AOL Network	26	EarthLink
2	Microsoft Sites	27	iWon.com
3	Yahoo!	28	Gator Network
4	Lycos	29	Colonize.com
5	Excite	30	iVillage
6	About.com Sites	31	Juno Online Services
7	Walt Disney Internet Group	32	GoTo
8	CNET Networks	33	CitySearch-Ticketmaster Online
9	Infospace Impressions	34	Bonzi.com
10	eBay	35	Snowball
11	Amazon	36	Coolsavings.com
12	AltaVista Network	37	Jobsonline.com
13	Time Warner Online	38	FortuneCity Network
14	NBCi	39	Network Commerce Inc.
15	LookSmart	40	Travelocity
16	Napster Digital*	41	News Corp. Online
17	The Uproar Network	42	American Greetings
18	eUniverse Network	43	BizRate.com
19	Ask Jeeves	44	Barnes & Noble
20	Viacom Online	45	Homestead.com
21	Real.com Network	46	Focalex.com
22	The Weather Channel	47	MyPoints Sites
23	Women.com Networks	48	NetZero Sites
24	AT&T Web Sites	49	ZMedia.com
25	Google.com	50	ClassMates.com Sites

Online and offline businesses and brands should not be separate entities, although commonly I have found that they are. Customers, whether they are using electronic channels, the phone or the high street do not differentiate between the brand and its proposition – their criteria for buying remains the same regardless of channel – 'Do I get what I came here for?'

CASE STUDY: DOTMUSIC

Creating the online brand

To highlight the risks, difficulties and approaches discussed in creating an online brand, let's take a look at online music retailer dotmusic, the UK's largest music web site offering news, reviews, multi-media clips on all genres and, of course, online purchasing of music.

dotmusic's challenge was how to grow their brand into the number one youth brand on the Internet and increase users from 740,000 to over 1.2 million. Their dilemma was how to create a recognized brand position amongst a wide and varying youth audience and gain 'first-mover' advantage over the competition. In assessing their brand, dotmusic discovered that they were suffering from credibility issues across the wide audience they served. They were also appealing to customers who acted emotionally to the brand, not rationally, meaning that the brand was likely to suffer from customer attrition very easily. They also discovered that the

Figure 4.3   dotmusic's home page at www.dotmusic.com

brand was competing with well-established offline brands that had moved online, such as high street music stores and radio stations and finally, that users of the dotmusic site were using it as an information-only vehicle and buying offline.

So what was the solution for dotmusic? First, dotmusic had to re-invent themselves. They created a new logo and developed a new strap line – 'what's your sound?' Then, they sought to develop an intelligent range of techniques for reaching their target audience, encompassing banner advertising online, WAP, TV, outdoor and press.

Their objectives were simple:

1. Create brand awareness

2. Communicate their brand values

3. Develop first mover advantage.

dotmusic's re-branding campaign saw them create personalities for users of the site, such as 'Jason' and 'Benji', that capitalized on the individuality and personality of music lovers.

By the end of the campaign in July 2000, dotmusic had increased its user base from 780,000 users to over 1.4 million, with awareness increasing to 38% recall, from its original 6% three months earlier.

4.5 Domain names

If you're starting out in e-business and do not have the base of a traditional brand to carry online, then choosing your eBrand needs careful planning and consideration. You need to think about the name of your e-business carefully, so that it is easy to find and remember. A good name can ensure your site is differentiated from the millions of others currently on the web.

One of the first steps in choosing your brand will be identifying whether it is available as a domain name. We'll explore this more later, but first, what is a domain name?

Your *domain name* or Uniform Resource Locator (URL) is your identity on the Internet – an easy-to-remember way of finding a computer connected to the Internet that contains your e-business site.

To be an e-business, you need a domain name that your customers can easily recognise and associate with your organization. Your domain name can be any combination of letters, words and numbers as long as it only uses lower-case letters (a–z) and the numbers 0–9. For example www.go123.com or www.shrinkingearth7.co.uk

Unfortunately, punctuation marks, spaces or other special characters cannot be used currently, with the exception of the hyphen (-). For example www.shrinking-earth.net. The key to a successful domain name is to make it short and easy to remember. Obviously, relevance to your business is important, as some people will often guess when trying to find a site by simply keying into the browser address bar a 'best-guess' based on words they naturally associate with the site they are looking for. This can result in lost traffic to competitors, or worse, frustrated customers who go elsewhere.

If the exact domain name you want is already registered, try variations on a theme. There are a variety of web sites you can visit to check the availability of domain names. InterNIC and Nominet control the allocation of domain names on the World Wide Web and both have web sites you can use to find companies that will register domain names for you. If you want to perform the checking yourself without involving a third party, such as your interactive

Figure 4.4   InterNIC web site – links to local sites to check and register domain names

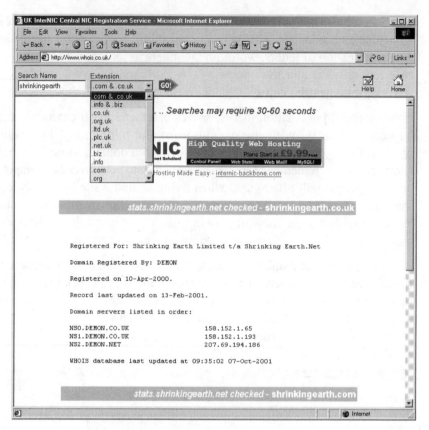

Figure 4.5   whois.co.uk – check your chosen domain name availability

advertising agency, sites like www.whois.co.uk are very useful. By entering the domain name you are looking for, followed by the domain suffix (for example, .com or .co.uk) it will perform a look-up on the database of registered domain names to see if it is available.

If it is, you can register it there and then. If not, you'll have to keep looking for alternatives.

Top level domain names

There are a variety of domain suffixes available. By far the most popular top-level domain is .com. Unfortunately, unless you registered your name early, most of the really good .com domains have already been taken. If you are based largely in the UK, a co.uk domain will serve you well.

Table 4.2   A Sample of some Country Domain Suffixes

.jp	for sites based in Japan
.fr	for sites based in France
.it	for sites based in Italy

Table 4.3   Some of Top-level Domain Suffixes

.com	originally for commercial sites based in the USA, but now more of a global domain
.org	generic, originally for non-profit organizations
.net	generic, originally for Internet and network organizations
.co.uk	for commercial sites based in the UK
.org.uk	for non-profit organizations in the UK

USEFUL WEB SITES   Referenced in this chapter

Dot-shopper survey	www.ebates.com
Cyberatlas	www.cyberatlas.com
Egg Online Bank	www.egg.com
Smile Interactive Bank	www.smile.co.uk
Dotmusic	www.dotmusic.com
Nominet	www.nominet.org
Internic	www.internic.com
Whois	www.whois.co.uk

CHAPTER SUMMARY

In this chapter, you have learnt:

1. The importance of developing the e-brand.

2. How to clearly identify your proposition and define your brand characteristics.

3. How to provide a better quality of service and an enhanced customer experience through more meaningful interaction.

4. That online branding is a fundamental activity undertaken by the business as a whole that will impact on every aspect of the customer life-cycle and relationship.

5. A brand is more than just a domain name.

TEST YOURSELF

1. The eBrand is vital to the success of your e-business as it one of the key methods most commonly used by new customers to find your web site.   *True or false?*

2. The key to e-business success is to throw as many marketing dollars at the brand as you can.   *True or false?*

3. Only 6% of customers are driven to e-business web sites through offline advertising.   *True or false?*

4. There are over 5 million individual web sites on the Internet today.   *True or false?*

5. The development of your e-business brand on the web is based purely on your ability to register a .com domain name.   *True or false?*

Chapter **5**

Customer loyalty
and the Internet

OVERVIEW

This chapter introduces you to the discussion of customer loyalty and the Internet. It reviews whether or not online customers are loyal and outlines ways in which your e-business can develop and measure levels of customer loyalty online.

We will also introduce you to an emerging loyalty strategy called 'content syndication' – the process of acquiring and re-packaging content to sell on or distribute to your customers to add value.

LEARNING OBJECTIVES

In this chapter, you will learn about:

- Customer loyalty on the Internet
- That evidence exists to suggest customer loyalty is achievable online
- How YOU can achieve customer loyalty via online channels
- The steps YOU must take to avoid customer attrition

Chapter Topic	Specific Learning Objective
5.0 Introduction	To understand the argument of whether customer loyalty exists online
5.1 Does loyalty exist online	To understand what influences customer loyalty
5.2 Let's look at the evidence	How existing online reward services operate
5.3 Ensuring customer retention	To understand the laws of online loyalty
5.4 Content Syndication	To understand content syndication – a loyalty strategy – how it could apply to your e-business and how to develop a loyalty strategy around it

KEYWORDS

Loyalty   Retention   eMarketplace   Syndication

Notepad exercises: 2

5.0 Introduction

In this chapter, we will tackle one of the longest running debates taking place in the online community. Does customer loyalty exist online? For some, the answer has to be yes, on the basis that traditional brands with established values and a lengthy heritage leverage those online, just as they do offline. For others, the answer is no, based on the fact that with so much choice and the Internet driving prices down, customers will buy from whichever site offers the best deal that day.

To get to the bottom of this argument, we will look at some of the facts and consider how YOU will need to integrate loyalty into your e-business strategy to ensure it avoids customer attrition and maintains customer retention.

Loyalty is the extent to which your customers continue to demonstrate behaviors, such as continuing to purchase from you, spending more with you and referring you on, when competitors offer more attractive prices, products, and/or services.

NOTEPAD EXERCISE

Write down five key reasons why customers buy from your web site.

5.1 Does loyalty exist online?

We all know that the cost of acquiring new customers far outweighs the cost of retaining existing customers. We also know that unless customers stick around and make lots of repeat purchases, profits will elude the e-business. So how can you tell if your online customers have loyalty towards your brand?

The online customer – buyer motivations

When it comes to buying online, purchasers, whether they are business-to-business or business-to-consumer, go for convenience, perceived quality and variety, or price. In the consumer sector, purchasers from many different market segments have different buying requirements and, although it is suggested that this group are amongst the most fickle on the Internet, once they find a site that continually meets their needs, they tend to stay with it. These are 'brand-loyal' buyers that tend to stay with a site if it continues to offer ease-of-use, convenience and choice. Amazon.com is a perfect example of this.

Most consumers that I have spoken with whilst researching the topic for this book said that when they purchased from Amazon and had a good experience, they will purchase again. And even those who didn't have a good experience said they will return to Amazon again later as Amazon had offered vouchers and jellies by way of compensation for their error. However, in other segments the primary driver is price. There are the 'bargain-hunter' buyers who are like sugar flies, hopping from supplier to supplier, looking for the best offers and the best prices. These are prolific users of auction sites and community sites such as www.letsbuyit.com that aggregate product pricing based on the number of buyers they can attract to a certain product. The more buyers bidding, the cheaper the unit price of the product gets. Finally, there is the 'Gourmet' segment. These customers purchase high value, branded goods. This category is less motivated by repetitive convenience, but instead seeks quality and will pay premium prices for premium products.

But what about the B2B market? If you sell to businesses, online loyalty is to play a different role for you. Customers are more likely to remain with a supplier if that supplier introduces *extranet* capabilities in the service mix offered, backed up by preferential/personalized pricing, improved trading terms and enhanced trading performance (such as order prioritization). Dell Computers was one of the early adopters of using extranets as a way of enhancing customer loyalty in the corporate sector.

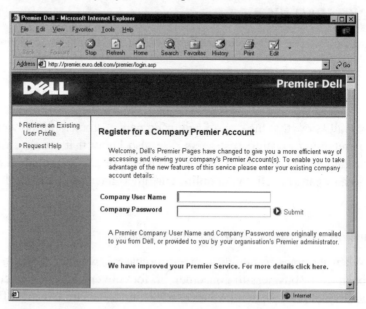

Figure 5.1   Dell's Premier account login page

Certainly, online loyalty looks like it will be big business. There are now several e-Loyalty schemes on the web that offer customers points or money in return for making purchases at specific web sites.

Tip: An Extranet is an extension of a company's network that is accessible to the outside world via a username and password. Extranets are usually provided to suppliers, customers or partners as a way of integrating them more closely into the business value chain. For further reading on Extranets, see Chapter 9.

5.2 Let's look at the evidence

Customer retention is fast becoming the preoccupation of many e-marketers. To address this, the Internet has spawned a whole new range of loyalty-based schemes and strategies. We'll take a look at these and evaluate them for their individual merits, but the cracks have already begun to show in the online world. Will online loyalty schemes, such as Web Rewards and Beenz survive? Maybe, but not in their current form, as Beenz has demonstrated. Let's take a quick look at two of the most well known on the Internet.

Web Rewards

WebRewards is an account-based scheme that can be offered by e-businesses to their customers. Purchasers can create an account and collect WebRewards immediately by purchasing at partner web sites, which are listed on the WebRewards site or are identified by the logo.

Collecting WebRewards involves transacting, or taking advantage of promotions or selected other online activities. When a transaction is completed at a Partner site, the account holder is asked to enter a unique Username and Password. Once this is verified, the account holder is then informed of the number of WebRewards they have collected. The WebRewards are automatically credited to the account immediately after the transaction. Account holders can then see a statement of their account at any time by visiting the WebRewards web site. The statement shows all the WebRewards earned and spent in the previous 6 months and where these can be redeemed. Already, WebRewards has over 100,000 users and is recruiting around 2,000 per day, making its customer database very valuable.

Beenz

Beenz was one of the first e-loyalty schemes designed to help web site owners manage their customer behaviour and customer relationships through incentive-based rewards programmes. Its proposition was (I say 'was' as Beenz ceased trading at the end of August 2001) to offer a marketing and customer relationship management (CRM) programme that offered the user and business

CUSTOMER LOYALTY AND THE INTERNET

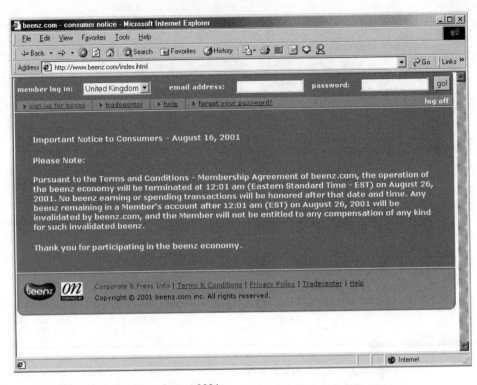

Figure 5.2   The beenz Web Site – August 2001

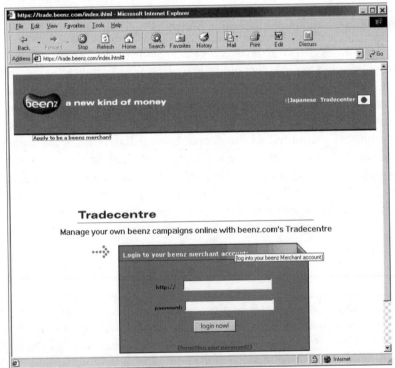

Figure 5.3   The beenz trade centre for e-businesses to measure campaigns

complete control, flexibility and value in the e-business space. Unfortunately for Beenz, points (or currency as they referred to it) wasn't enough to encourage shoppers online and to the sites that signed-up for it.

Beenz was designed to be a universal currency on the web. Until the end of August, Beenz points could be earned and spent globally with no geographical restrictions, which made it a very appealing loyalty programme to organizations that have multiple sites for different countries they trade in. It also meant that beenz could be traded anywhere on the web. Beenz saw itself as an attractive global marketing tool for e-businesses and consumers, offering site owners a highly focused yet relatively inexpensive way to attract consumers to their web sites, increase sales, develop long-term relationships and stimulate continuing interest in their products and services. Beenz operated in a similar way to Web Rewards, by enabling online purchasers to create an account at beenz.com and wherever they saw the beenz logo displayed on a web site, they knew that by spending there they would accrue more beenz. beenz could then be traded in at a later date against products or services from any of the beenz merchants.

From the e-business merchant perspective, access to the beenz trade centre provided access to real-time data on campaigns being run that utilized the beenz currency. For example, if an e-business wished to incentivize customers to buy online through its site, it could give away a quantity of beenz to each customer, which would then be traded in against purchases made. Through the beenz trade centre, the e-business can monitor and measure the performance of their campaign to see how it is doing.

So what wrong for beenz and why, when incentive programmes such as Air Miles, one of the world's oldest, continues to prosper? Part of the answer lies in the fact that customers will be loyal online, but not for the incentive of points. Their motivators are far greater than that and are based around service, convenience, choice, quality and price. e-Businesses, such as eBay and Dell, are harnessing web technologies to deliver these loyalty benefits to their customers through customization and personalization, customer-specific extranets and content.

5.3 Ensuring customer retention

 So let's have a look at some of the ways in which your e-business can harness web technology to deliver the kind of benefits customers want and you need to offer to ensure their continued loyalty.

e-Business sites are still failing buyers

It is estimated that at least four out of five online purchasers have experienced one failed purchase and 28 percent of all online purchases fail. Why is providing good customer service online so difficult to achieve?

at least 4 out of 5 online purchasers have experienced a failed purchase

Here are some of the reasons why e-business site lose customers:

- Speed – Many sites take too long to load;
- Design – Many sites are badly designed, making it difficult for users to find the products or services they are interested in;
- Robust – Many sites suffer from technical problems, including forms or the order function not working, or pages and images missing;
- Service – Finally, many sites simply lack the logistical and fulfilment infrastructure they need to perform e-business effectively.

THE LAWS OF CUSTOMER LOYALTY

Online

- Rewards help, but they do not buy customer loyalty.
- Loyalty should be a two-way process – loyalty towards customers is easily facilitated online and will encourage customers to be loyal to the e-business in return.
- Loyalty is based on trust.
- Loyalty is a personal thing – one customer's loyalty may be different to another.
- Not all customers are made equal – an effective loyalty programme treats them as individuals and rewards them accordingly.
- Loyalty programmes should not be over-marketed – this can lead to disappointment and expectations being raised that can't be met.
- Your best and most loyal customers are those that have already used the channel – concentrate on them first.

In e-business

- A long-term, strategic approach to customer relationships.
- A value proposition not a short-term promotion.

In summary, customer loyalty on the Internet is difficult to achieve. You are competing against multiple factors that will drive customers away. These factors include price transparency, ease of customer switching at the click of a mouse and wide-ranging choice. What you need is a strategy that keeps customers coming back.

Failed purchases deter repeat visits and repeat purchases. For many, a bad experience or a frustrating visit will result in that potential customer not re-visiting that e-business site again.

To avoid customer attrition, we should look to ensure that we can deliver content to the customer's screen quickly and effectively. Research has shown that the average Internet user expects to wait no longer than 10–15 seconds for a Home Page to load; five minutes to find the product or service they want and 4–5 minutes to complete the order. Anything over six days in terms of fulfilment, and customers will be put off buying from the site again. So, to avoid attrition and ensure retention, the site must be well designed, robust and well integrated into business processes to ensure a high quality of customer experience.

NOTEPAD EXERCISE

Write down five key ways you could create loyalty via your web site.

For further reading on online customer loyalty – an excellent report from ActivMedia Research, published in March 2000 can be purchased from www.activmediaresearch.com/capturing_online_markets.html

5.4 Content syndication – a loyalty strategy?

On the web, customers are faced with infinite choice, often leaving them dazed and confused. How does the average e-business overcome this confusion and provide an ongoing meaningful experience? Content syndication is one of the emerging business models on the web that seeks to address the issue of customer retention head on.

Successful content syndication delivers the right information, at the right time, in the right format to the right customer.

To be successful, e-businesses need to keep customers and other online trading partners up-to-date with timely, relevant, and compelling content. Such content may include product information, late-breaking discounts and offers, news articles, rich media such as audio and video files, or even applications such as calculators or wizards.

Content Syndication is the process of acquiring or reusing information in a different format and adding value to it in unique ways and then reselling or distributing it to serve the needs of different customer groups.

The easiest way to describe content syndication is to look at the news publishing sector. For example, www.moreover.com collects news and articles in electronic format from over 3000 different sources and redistributes it to many thousands more sites that need up-to-date news for their varying customer audiences.

In the world of content, there are three primary roles an e-business can play:

1. An *originator* – a business that creates content, such as news publishers.

2. A *syndicator* – a business that collects and packages content, adds value to it and then re-sells it on.

3. A *distributor of content* – a business that acquires content at a relatively low cost and uses it to enhance the value it offers to it users/customer, such as www.shrinkingearth.net.

So how does your e-business develop a syndication strategy? Involving your e-business in content syndication will require a change of role to one of these.

So you developed and implemented your loyalty strategy, now how do you measure its contribution? There are five key performance indicators.

---

5 KEY MEASURES　　　　**Customer loyalty in e-business**

- Repeat behaviour

- Average time spent on site (stickiness)

- Recency and frequency of purchases

- Customers ignore competitive offers

- Referral rates increase.

USEFUL WEB SITES	Referenced in this chapter
Let's buy it	www.letsbuyit.com
Dell	www.premier.euro.dell.com
Beenz	www.beenz.com
Web Rewards	www.webrewards.com
shrinking earth.net	www.shrinkingearth.net
Moreover	www.moreover.com
ActivMedia Research	www.activemediaresearch.com

CHAPTER SUMMARY

In this chapter, you have learnt that:

1. Online customers will repeat purchase from suppliers that offer **choice**, **convenience**, **quality** and **price**.

2. Your customers' loyalty is under threat from issues such as price transparency, ease of customer switching and wide-ranging choice, all facilitated through the Internet.

3. There are seven principle laws in online customer loyalty: It's **two-way**; it's based on **trust**; it's **specific**; it's **personal**; all customers are not **equal**; over-marketing loyalty programmes can create a mismatch in **expectation** vs **deliverable**; your **best customers** should be your primary concern.

4. Through harnessing web technologies to offer personalization, customization, content and customer-specific extranets, you are more likely to win customer loyalty.

5. Content syndication is a possible loyalty strategy for your e-business, but requires a subtle change in direction to deliver it.

TEST YOURSELF

1. *Loyalty* means 'the extent to which your customers demonstrate behaviours, such as repeat purchase from you, spending more with you and referring you on, when competitors offer more attractive prices, products, and/or services'. *True or false?*

2. Rewards schemes are by far the most effective method of creating loyalty than using web technologies to offer personalized and customized online experiences. *True or false?*

3. Four out of five customers experience a failed online transaction that deters them later from returning to that site to purchase. *True or false?*

4. Customer loyalty initiatives are short-term activities designed to acquire customers, not long-terms strategies designed to grow contribution and profitability. *True or false?*

5. Content syndication is the process of acquiring and re-packaging content to sell on or distribute to your customers. *True or false?*

Chapter **6**

Developing best practice in e-business strategy

OVERVIEW

In this chapter, we look at best practice in e-business and attempt to answer the following questions: How do you create a high quality of experience online for your customers? What are the legal obligations being imposed by law on e-businesses and where can you turn for help at an international level? Developing best practice in e-business strategy introduces you to the 'three M' framework, a planning tool that enables you to consider the various issues of online trading channels, marketing to your customers and then transacting with them.

LEARNING OBJECTIVES

In this chapter you will learn about:

- How to develop YOUR strategy to embrace best practice in e-business;
- The various guidelines and legislation being developed for e-business;
- The various industry associations in e-business that exist at an International level.

Chapter Topic	Specific Learning Objective
1.0 Introduction	To understand the importance of e-Business Best Practice
1.1 e-Business Best Practice	To understand the impact of QofCE
1.2 Legal Guidelines	How to understand the application of legal guidelines
1.3 Information Sources	How to locate relevant e-business information and industry associations

KEYWORDS

Best Practice   QofCE   Legislation   Three M Framework

Notepad exercises: 2

6.0 Introduction

In approaching best practice in e-business, you must look at the bigger picture. The e-business of the future will not just concern itself with the Internet, but will extend across multiple digital channels, including Interactive TV (iTV) and mobile devices, such as smart phones and Personal Digital Assistants (PDAs). Each of these channels will become complementary to each other, not competitive. Your e-business strategy must be able manage the process of moving content and customers across all these platforms. Different channels require different rules, but more about that and 'content re-purposing' later in Chapter 7. In this chapter, we will look at best practice e-business and discuss specifically how to develop a 'high quality of experience' for online customers, together with some of the legal guidelines you will need to consider when developing your strategy. We will also look at some of the industry associations you can turn to for further support and advice, on an International level.

NOTEPAD EXERCISE

Write down the various channels through which your organization currently sells to customers. How do you create trust and an effective experience of your brand through these channels and what techniques do you use?

6.1 e-Business best practice

Best practice in e-business is based on one main criterion, which I call the Quality of the Customer Experience (QofCE). To develop best practice in e-business, *you* must first determine what *your* customer wants from you – whether a particular aspect of e-business is offered or not, for example.

You must ask yourself the following questions:

- Is this feature, content or functionality actually something that my customers will appreciate and use? Will it retain customers longer and make them more profitable?

- Will my customers like this capability and come back to use it again and again, or will they get frustrated and abandon it for a competing site?

Best practice in e-business is about knowing how important the customer experience is to your strategy.

A good evaluation of how to begin developing best practice in e-business is by asking questions such as:

- What are my strategic objectives for e-business?

- Who are my target customers; what are their objectives, needs and goals?

- Does our e-business help our customers accomplish their goals *and* our company's goals?

- Does my customer experience something quick and easy to use that will bring them back and keep them from going to competitors?

The customer experience is greatly affected by many tactical aspects online and these are the main criteria by which best practice in e-business is judged.

NOTEPAD EXERCISE

See if you can answer the questions I have posed above by writing down your thoughts on your organization's e-business capability.

What is Quality of Customer Experience (QofCE)?

More and more Internet users in both Business-to-Business and Business-to-Consumer, with minimal technical expertise, are using online channels to purchase products and services, from known and unknown brands. As a result, customers demand accessible, fast and easy-to-use e-business solutions. The web is one of the few mediums that makes switching to a competitor fast, cheap and as easy as typing in a new web address.

Sites that generate the best quality of customer experience capture the more 'sticky' traffic, achieve higher revenues and build stronger brand values and awareness. In contrast, the sites with poor quality of customer experience, including those with the best back-end technology or a great off-line brand, lose customers and revenue at an astonishing rate.

Sites that generate the best Quality of Customer Experience capture the more 'sticky' traffic, achieve higher revenues and build stronger brand values and awareness.

To better understand the concept of quality of customer experience, remember the 'three M' framework:

Medium — Online channels are constrained: mobile phones, PDA, PC and TV screens are relatively small; modems can be slow; users are technically inexperienced. Despite the hype about the future of online channels, the true way to succeed in e-business is to create customer experiences that work within the constraints of the channel.

Marketing – The Internet has changed the rules of effective marketing. Most importantly, on the web, 'brand' is the experience and the experience is the brand. The rules of engagement have changed and permission, coupled to trust, (see Chapter 10) is the key to success.

Money – If customers can't buy, they won't buy. Make it easy for the customer to give you money.

To succeed in e-business, you must endeavour to create a high Quality of Customer Experience.

Here are my tips for factors your e-business must address to support a good QofCE:

1. Promote comfort – offer secure online ordering.

It is important that your e-business communicates to its customers that buying online from your site is safe and secure. This helps to promote comfort and instil confidence, whilst ensuring that customers return and make repeat purchases.

2. Confirm orders received by e-mail.

Ensure that the site is set-up to confirm back to a customer, by e-mail, their order details. This promotes a sense of confidence from the customer that their order has been received and is being dealt with. Make sure, however, that you do not confirm back to the customer any information relating to their credit card details.

3. Fulfilment.

Finally, ensure you deliver on time, every time. One of the biggest reasons for customer attrition on the web is due to not being able to deliver on time. If you quote delivery timescales, stick to them. In addition, always ensure that delivery charges are well identified to the customer upfront and at the point of purchase.

6.2 Legal guidelines

To do e-business, utilizing different digital channels, requires you to be aware of the legal implications of doing so. I am not a lawyer, but I want to offer you some insight into the current state of play in relation to online legislation. Currently, there remain many areas of uncertainty relating to online law, due partly to the fact that the legal profession had lagged behind the technology, and partly due to e-business knowing no national boundaries and creating situations that haven't existed in the past. As late as autumn 1999 there was still no specific Internet legislation. However, that has all changed during 2000 and 2001 with the arrival of several new pieces of legislation, including the Electronic Communications Act and the European Commissions eCommerce Directive, which comes into force in January 2002. The Directive will impose 'additional' information requirements on all web sites operating in the EU and will (in most, if not all cases) require the modification of existing eCommerce procedures to ensure contracts are validly formed online. It will also subject e-businesses to new rules on the sending of junk e-mail. On the controversial issue of service providers' liability for illegal content – be it child pornography, pirate copyright material or defamation, it may lay the foundations for a new 'notice and takedown' regime, giving both Internet Service Providers and injured parties a clearer picture of where they stand.

Here are the highlights of these important legal changes. But take my advice first, whatever e-business or e-marketing activity you are planning, get some good legal advice at a local level to where that activity takes place.

1. Establish the rules of engagement

Your e-business site must set out your Terms and Conditions of Business for everyone, clearly and upfront. This will set the stage for transactions conducted on your site and will establish which local laws your site is covered under.

2. Privacy and data protection

To ensure transparency and boost consumer confidence, e-businesses that promote and sell their services online will need to make available certain general information about themselves, their activities and relevant authorizations in an 'easily, directly and permanently accessible form'. This comes hot on the heels of the new requirements imposed by the Distance Selling Regulations last year (see www.olswang.com/ecommerce/legal_news/distance_ sales.htm).

Draft regulations will be published after the consultation, in the light of which all businesses providing or advertising their services online (not just those currently subject to the Distance Selling Regulations) will need to audit their web sites for compliance. As yet, it is unclear whether there will be criminal penalties for breach of the new information requirements.

3. When is a contract not a contract?

The new legislation will impact the way in which contracts are formed online and will require an e-business to audit its web site and sales procedures. The Directive specifies information that must be provided to individuals to allow them to understand easily how they should place orders online. This includes the technical steps to follow to conclude the contract; the extent to which the contract will be fulfilled by the e-business and whether it will be accessible, as well as the technical means for identifying and correcting input errors and the languages offered for the conclusion of the contract. This information must be readily accessible. If it is not, the e-business' contracts with its customers may be void. The changes may well affect the technical way in which the e-business accepts and confirms orders. For example, it may specify whether the site uses 'I accept' buttons, automatic e-mail confirmations, dynamic page responses, etc.

At an international level, a global code for eCommerce is being developed by business organizations on either side of the Atlantic, who are working together on a set of global standards to promote consumer confidence in online transactions. European businesses must, of course, not lose sight of their other obligations under legislation, such as the Distance Selling Directive and Unfair Terms Regulations. The organizations concerned are BBB Online (part of the US Better Business Bureau), Eurochambres, an association of European chambers of commerce, and FEDMA, which represents European direct-marketing businesses. The three are planning to harmonize their codes of conduct to provide a voluntary, international standard for online commerce, as well as a dispute resolution framework.

Participating e-businesses will be able to subscribe to benchmarks for reliability, truthful advertising, customer privacy and customer service, in return for the use of a 'trustmark' on their web site. The three groups have said they hope to have the trustmark programme established by early 2002. Various kitemark schemes and accreditation schemes already exist at a national and international level. In the UK, these include schemes like Trust UK, the IMRG Hallmark and the Which? Web Trader scheme. The new international trustmark aims to overcome some of the difficulties raised by differences in national laws on a range of issues such as privacy and dispute resolution.

NOTEPAD EXERCISE

If your organization has a web presence, write down five key elements of the site that meet existing e-business best practice and promote comfort.

6.3 Information sources and industry associations

There are several authoritative industry associations that you can use either for information gathering or to become members of as part of your e-business strategy. These include:

The Interactive Media in Retail Group

The IMRG are possibly one of the longest established e-business industry associations and boast many of the biggest names in media, retailing, technology and consultancy as members (including my own company, shrinking earth.net). The IMRG's web site, at www.imrg.org, is information rich, containing reports, surveys, news and more. Of most importance is that The IMRG has produced a Code of Practice for e-business, designed to set out how responsible online businesses should conduct themselves. The code has recently been updated. For the latest version, please visit the site.

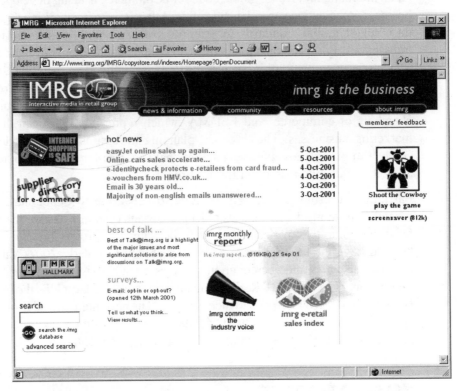

Figure 6.1   The IMRG web site home page

eCentre UK

eCentre UK are a collaboration of the Article Number Association and the eBusiness Association, designed to help businesses that already have a heavy investment in Electronic Data Interchange based systems, to embrace e-business. eCentre UK currently have 150,000 members, 90% of which are small to medium-sized enterprises and collaborate with other industry associations such as the IMRG. They also collaborate with government agencies such as the DTi on the subject of e-business. However, it should be noted that eCentre UK are heavily biased toward the manufacturing industry and are specifically useful when helping to integrate e-business into production processes involving bar coding, etc.

For more information, visit eCentre UK at www.e-centre.org.uk.

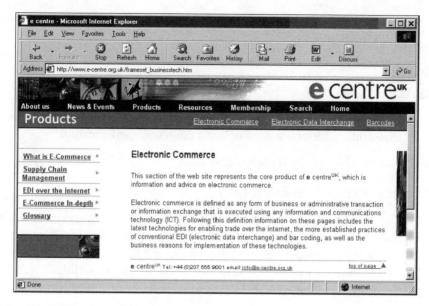

Figure 6.2   eCentre UK web site home page

International organizations

At an international level, e-business associations and forums worth checking out include:

European eCommerce Association

The European eCommerce Association (EEA) is a non-profit consortium of companies committed to promoting and developing e-business and online trading in Europe. Member companies include some of the leading names from a diverse cross-section of industries, including hardware and software manufacturers, financial institutions, integrators, Internet service providers, publishers, event organisers, recruitment companies, consultants, research organizations and retailers.

The address is: www.eeauk.com

Venture Capital Institute

VCI is sponsored by the National Association of Small Business Investment Companies and the National Venture Capital Association, and has been around for over 25 years.

The address is: http://www.vcinstitute.org/

TRUSTe

TRUSTe is an award-winning organization that seeks to ensure privacy rights on the web. This site gives excellent and detailed guidelines on how to ensure that your customers will take comfort in the fact that their private information will remain private.

The address is: http://www.truste.org

DISA

The DISA web site offers information on data interchange efforts, including glossaries, tutorials, workshops and conference information.

The address is: http://www.disa.org/

Electronic Commerce Institute

The ECInstitute is made up of trade associations, user groups and academic institutions, and is devoted to education and certification for EC professionals. The website's content is still a bit sparse, but contains extensive information on EC Institute members and its board that might be useful.

The address is   http://www.ecinstitute.org/

The Online Privacy Alliance

The Online Privacy Alliance is a diverse group of corporations whose goal it is to secure and enhance the privacy of consumers and their individual rights to privacy.

The address is: http://www.privacyalliance.org

Shop.org

Shop.org is an online knowledge exchange for Web retailers. Stemming from the National Retail Federation, Shop.org boasts over 400 members, and is a repository for many articles, papers, and other information that pertains to the field of online selling.

The address is: http://www.shop.org

eLab: Electronic Commerce Research Laboratory

The eLab, founded in 1994 by Professors Donna Hoffman and Tom Novak at Vanderbilt, is one of the only facilities devoted entirely to e-commerce research. The site offers online access to research reports, sponsor information and details about current projects. Summer 2001, the lab is working on the eLab Infrastructure Project.

The address is: http://www2000.ogsm.vanderbilt.edu/index.html

Privacy Foundation

The purpose of the Privacy Foundation is to educate the public on communications technologies and services that may pose a threat to personal privacy. The web site contains up-to-date news, privacy advisories and reports written by Privacy Foundation researchers, a glossary, FAQs and links to other resources. Although applicable to the home PC-user, the site's content also extends to the enterprise environment.

The address is: http://www.privacyfoundation.org/index.cfm

USEFUL WEB SITES **Referenced in this chapter**

Interactive Media & Retail Group	www.imrg.org
eCentre	www.e-centre.org.uk
shrinking earth	www.shrinkingearth.net
Olswang	www.olswang.com

CHAPTER SUMMARY

In this chapter you have learnt:

1. That one of the most important factors in e-business is to ensure you can offer a High Quality of Customer Experience across all channels.

2. That the three M framework is a useful planning tool for e-business strategy: Medium – remember the constraints of the channels; Marketing – remember the requirements upon you to gain your customer's permission to talk to them online and build trust at every stage; Money – make it easy for customers to transact with you. Don't build barriers to repeat business.

3. That new legislation is being developed all the time and it is your responsibility to make sure that your e-business strategy embraces and adheres to the law.

4. That there are plenty of sources of reference to e-business best practice internationally. Use their knowledge and experience to gain competitive advantage in your market.

TEST YOURSELF

1. The three M framework stands for Money, Men and Moments of Interactivity. *True or false?*

2. e-Business best practice is firmly based on ensuring customers receive a high quality of experience from the brand, regardless of which channel they use. *True or false?*

3. The web is one of the few channels that makes switching suppliers for online customers difficult. *True or false?*

4. e-Business is global, but the law is inherently local. Good e-businesses should seek legal advice at a local level of activity as well as an overall strategic level. *True or false?*

5. A new initiative is being introduced by e-business associations across the world to bring in to place a global standard for online trading that is designed to engender trust from Internet buyers through standard codes of conduct for e-businesses. *True or false?*

Chapter **7**

Best practice
e-marketing

OVERVIEW

This chapter introduces you to the world of e-marketing. It helps you discover what e-marketing is all about as well as the tools and techniques that comprise the e-marketing mix. It also focuses on best practice e-marketing, explaining how to develop and implement effective e-mail, member-get-member and online advertising campaigns, using devices such HTML e-mail, virals, banners, pop-ups, micro-sites and more.

LEARNING OBJECTIVES

In this chapter, you will learn about:

- Using e-mail marketing to drive customers to your e-business
- The various new media channels
- How to use these channels in a business & marketing context

Chapter Topic	Specific Learning Objective
7.0 Introduction	
7.1 The e-marketing mix	e-Mail and how to develop an e-mail campaign
7.2 Viral marketing	How to develop and use viral marketing
7.3 Banner advertising and pop-ups	Online advertising and how to use it
7.4 Micro sites	What they are and how to use them
7.5 Content and the multi-channel marketing environment	How to adapt content for different e-marketing channels

KEYWORDS

e-Mail	Viral marketing	Banners	Micro sites
Content	Multi-channel		

Notepad exercises: 1

7.0 Introduction

As e-business strategies evolve, astute companies will begin to realize that the key to their future success does not solely lie in how technically competent they are or how much bandwidth they own. The key will be how well do they know and understand their customers.

Bandwidth is the amount of data your connection (or channel) to the Internet can handle at any one time.

Marketing databases are becoming a precious commodity and the successful 'e' brand will become the guardians of this data. As a result of the Internet, we are now able to amass detailed important information on our customers, which we can use to mine and deliver a more personalized, interactive experience.

But what's this got to do with best practice in e-marketing? Well, quite simply, much of the e-marketing effort is designed to drive traffic to the site and create 'sticky' content that will ensure customers return time and time again. Therefore, knowing our customers and what they want and need will be critical to achieving this.

There now exists a wide range of promotional mechanics designed to drive traffic, build awareness or capture customer data.

Mechanics are tools used for online marketing. Examples would include banner adverts, pop-ups and e-mail.

 7.1 e-Mail marketing

Electronic mail (e-mail) is described as the Internet's killer application for marketers. It is one of the most popular features of the Internet and has become a part of everyday life for millions of people. e-Mail is a successful, cost-effective means of communicating with customers and developing customer loyalty. Recent surveys by e-marketer.com show that 65% percent of companies spend between 1% and 5% of their marketing budgets on e-mail marketing, with an additional 22% spending in excess of 5%. Therefore, 87% of companies believe that e-mail marketing is very important to their marketing strategy.

Benefits of e-mail marketing

Outbound e-mail sent to customers who voluntarily elect to receive marketing messages from a company ('opt-in' e-mail) drives traffic.

BEST PRACTICE EMARKETING

The importance of e-mail as a marketing tool is increasing due to its many strengths. The e-mail audience is large and growing, with e-mail the preferred method by which many people wish to be contacted. e-Mail facilitates an integrated approach to online marketing. There are two types of e-mail – sophisticated messages that look like web pages, called *HTML* e-mail and *Plain text*. Both are used for slightly different applications and have different issues associated with them. Plain text messages are generally used to send content-heavy newsletters or communications, and HTML messages can be used to send more complex and compelling communications.

THE 5 KEY BENEFITS OF e-MAIL MARKETING

- e-mail can deliver customized and personalized content based on customer preferences.

- e-mail can be 10 times as cost-effective as traditional direct mail due to the elimination of postage and printing costs.

- An e-mail campaign can be executed in a matter of days and customers can receive a message almost instantaneously, leading to response times measured in hours, not weeks.

- e-mail significantly outperforms traditional direct mail in response and conversion rates.

- e-mail campaigns can collect vast amounts of useful data that can be used to refine and better target future campaigns.

People use e-mail to communicate every day. This means that if the customers you want to reach are not using e-mail already, chances are they soon will be.

Some facts and figures about e-mail

- In 1999, the number of e-mail accounts reached over 570 million. By then end of 2001, reports state that there will be more than 1 billion e-mail accounts worldwide.

- In 2000, over 7 trillion e-mail messages were sent.

- In 2002, worldwide e-mail volume is expected to reach over 576 million messages sent per day.

The number of commercial e-mail messages that the average online user will receive per year will increase 40 times from around 40 messages in 1999 to more than 1,600 in 2005.

Integrated marketing brings a range of media activities together. Sending the right message at the right time, using the right channel. e-Mail complements such efforts by performing essential functions such as those historically serviced by traditional marketing channels, including:

- Information dissemination
- Special offers and promotions
- Interaction
- Branding

But remember, for e-mail to be effective, it must be:

- Targeted
- Relevant
- Personalized

Most active e-mail marketing businesses seek to develop a 'permission-based' e-mail marketing list comprising of customers and visitors to their web site who sign up (or 'opt-in') to receive information, news, updates or/and special offers. Creating an opt-in list ensures marketers have 'permission' to target a self-selected audience who are interested in receiving messages from your company. Over time, a company will gain more detailed information about the preferences and buying habits of each customer. Analysis of this data allows more finely personalized products and offers to be sent which increases response rates. This data can also be used to identify and reward the most loyal customers with personalized offers. Effective e-mail must include an 'unsubscribe' or 'opt-out' option. This is not only best practice, but has become a legal requirement in some jurisdictions.

e-mail marketing is highly cost-effective

e-mail marketing is NOT free. There are costs associated with the creation and production of e-mail messages – such as copy, and if using HTML, then graphics. However, e-mail is still very economical. Furthermore, much of the cost of communicating by e-mail is transferred to the customer or the Internet. The resulting savings mean that e-mail messages can cost only pennies apiece. Generally, e-mail marketers can expect to pay between £0.01 and £0.25 per e-mail. Low implementation costs and ongoing cost-effectiveness also mean an e-mail campaign can involve more frequent communication with customers, such as a weekly newsletter, allowing the marketer to develop an ongoing relationship with the customer.

Speed: fast implementation and rapid response

e-mail can be set-up and executed in a matter of hours, compared to a lead-time of two to four months for direct mail. Response times are fast, too: Typically 80% of responses to an e-mail campaign are received in the first 48 hours. Rapid response rates make e-mail especially attractive to marketers accustomed to waiting weeks or even months for the results of a direct mail campaign. Fast turnaround of an e-mail campaign can ensure you beat the competition, test alternative messages and changing messages or offers on the fly as circumstances or customer feedback dictate. Fast implementation, combined with real-time responses, make it possible to test an e-mail with a small sample group before launching the full campaign and adjust content to improve results.

Higher response rates

A Forrester Research study found that e-mail marketing typically generates a click-through of 10–20%. This is impressive compared to a successful direct mail response rate of 1–3%. Likewise, click-through rates are much higher for opt-in e-mail than for banner advertising, for which click-through rates have fallen to 0.05% or less. Conversion rates of web site visitors to buyers as a result of e-mail deliver, on average, 5% higher results. Some individual campaigns can produce significantly higher rates, depending on the effectiveness of the content.

Rich-media HTML e-mail, like those opposite, with dynamic or static graphics in the message, can deliver even higher response rates. In one survey, companies that executed HTML e-mail campaigns reported that, on average, click-through rates doubled over text-only e-mail. One retail company reported getting a 10% click-through rate with text messages and a response rate that increased to 24% with graphical HTML messages. HTML is emerging as a popular format for e-mail marketing, as more e-mail software packages (such as Lotus Notes and Microsoft Outlook) and web-based e-mail services (Hotmail) support HTML messages. However, it is important to keep the customer in mind, and recognise that not all recipients want to receive HTML e-mail. In B2B, most companies ask customers to select their preferred format: text-only or HTML.

Measurability of results

e-mail offers marketers unprecedented measuring and testing for virtually every aspect of the campaign. Analysis of the resulting data helps to better target future campaigns. Measurement can take place immediately and enable a fast response. e-Mail marketing is particularly well suited for testing and research,

Figure 7.1   HTML e-mail from Tony Stone Images

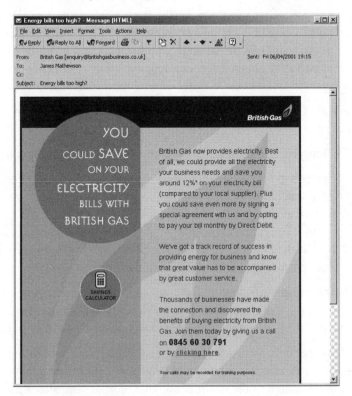

Figure 7.2   An HTML e-mail from British Gas

through the use of web address (URL) tracking and back-end records; results can be collected soon after an e-mail campaign has been sent.

One powerful tool for gathering data is 'redirect URLs'. Each individual recipient's e-mail message contains a unique click-through address, so that when the customer clicks on the link, tracking software records this customer's response. A report detailing the number of customer responses can then be generated for the marketing team to analyze. While collecting valuable data, the process remains transparent to the customer. e-Mail response data can then be combined with recorded information about the customer's actions, either at the web site, or from data gathered from other sources to build a detailed profile for each customer. Individual profiles can then be analyzed to chart factors such as customer profitability, revenue generation, timing and frequency, plus review customer affinity for various products and demographic variables. All of this information helps in planning future e-mail campaigns.

Four steps for developing a targeted e-mail campaign

Developing an effective e-mail campaign requires the following processes to be covered.

1. Data Collection – before you can begin to run effective e-mail campaigns, you must first have a list. By far the best practice way to achieve this is to build your own list by capturing customer or visitor e-mail addresses directly, either at the point of sale, through web forms, via sales staff, over the phone, etc. Naturally, of course, you can rent lists, but experience has proved that rented data is less effective than building your own mailing list.

2. e-Mail Composition – writing the e-mail requires an understanding of two things:

1. What type of e-mail can the recipients receive (plain text or HTML?)

2. What call to action will they best respond to (offer, promotion, incentive?). Once you have decided on what your e-mail message is going to say, the next step is to write the copy, keeping it short, sharp and the call to action (normally a hyperlink) visible and close to the beginning of the e-mail. If the e-mail is to be HTML based, there will also be some graphics production and HTML programming required as well.

3. Distribution – following the composition stage, the e-mail then has to be distributed to your e-mail list. This is normally performed by a list server – an automated software application that sends out the e-mail in bulk.

4. Measurement – finally, having distributed your e-mail message to your target list, the next step is to record how many click-throughs there have been from the message to the destination page of your web site or micro site, or if there is a freefone telephone number, how many calls the e-mail generated.

Developing a campaign

The timescale for developing and implementing a e-mail campaign can be anything from an afternoon to several weeks, depending on the requirements of the campaign and whether you are using plain text or HTML e-mail. Costs for e-mail can vary from campaign to campaign subject to the execution used. Plain text e-mail can be written and distributed in an afternoon and in bulk for less than a penny an e-mail. HTML could take longer and therefore be more expensive.

Let's assume your campaign involves sending out 10,000 e-mails at a cost per e-mail of 15 pence, totalling £1,500.00 (this cost includes composition and distribution). From that initial 10,000, you achieve a response of 12%, providing you with a total response of 1200 customers. The cost per response can be calculated at £1.25; 5% of those respondents go on to purchase from your e-business site, totalling 60 sales. The cost per sale can therefore be identified as £25. With an average order value of £60, the campaign delivers a Return On Investment of £2,100 profit and £3,600 in total sales.

Naturally, there is the cost of any incentive to be included, but on the whole, this model demonstrates targeted e-mail to be a highly effective method of marketing and sales.

Figure 7.3   The Return On Investment (ROI) Model for e-mail

Best practice e-mail marketing

Comparison Chart for B2B and B2C e-mail

B2B	B2C
Avoid HTML e-mail	Use HTML but keep file size down
Keep text brief & to the point	Incentivize the e-mail offer
Use links as call to actions	Provide links & a freefone number
Personalize the e-mail	Personalize the e-mail
Use the community's language	Use jargon-free language
Send your message out mid-week	Send your message out on Fridays
Provide an opt-out mechanism	Provide an opt-out mechanism

7.2 Viral marketing

Viral marketing is a method of online promotion that relies on your message being passed from person to person without your direct involvement. Viral gets its name from the way viruses are spread by person-to-person e-mails, multiplying at every stage.

Viral campaigns can be a highly effective method in e-marketing of driving traffic to your web site, achieving brand awareness or promoting a specific product, service or event.

Viral campaigns work by using subject matter that is either useful to your target audience or highly entertaining. Figure 7.5 demonstrates a viral campaign that was purely designed to spread the word through entertainment, while Figure 7.4 was a useful tool aimed at the avid football fan. The objective is to create a message that people will want to pass on to their friends, family and/ or colleagues. By avoiding gimmicks but creating a stir, this sharing process can give your viral campaign longevity and cost-effectiveness.

One of the most popular viral campaigns performed was Frog Bender by Joe Cartoon.com (www.joecartoon.com). This entertaining viral application has probably now been around the world several times and reached the inbox of ten of thousands of recipients.

Figure 7.4 A useful viral – the Euro 2000 competition planner produced by Oasis Communications (www.oasis.com)

*Figure 7.5   An entertaining viral – The
Frog Bender by Joe Cartoon
(www.joecarton.com)*

CASE STUDY: FT.COM

FT.com, the online publishing arm of the Financial Times, recently ran a
viral campaign designed to achieve several key objectives. These included:

● Drive traffic to FT.com

● Build brand awareness of FT.com

● Drive new user registrations to the site

● Build profiles on their user base

● Bring lapsed users back to the site

● Maximize their learning from viral media and the messages usedThe
campaign was supported by banner adverts designed to drive users to
the FT.com web site, where they could interact with the viral on the
site or download it and send it to colleagues and friends. To attract
users, the campaign was also incentivized with a prize.

Figure 7.6   FT.com banner ad that supported the viral campaign

On arrival to the site, users were asked to register to download and play
the game – this registration process offered FT two things – (1) the
player's details and (2) referral details.

So did it work? Well, yes! The game concept encouraged high user
interaction, which, coupled to the range of audio banners used to drive
traffic, it achieved impact and gave the FT.com brand a much wider
appeal. The fun element of the game coupled to the prize incentive
removed any obstacles to user registration and the overall campaign
increased visitor dwell time on the FT.com site to more than ten minutes

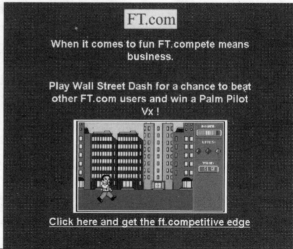

Figure 7.7   FT.com's viral game –
Registration Page

Figure 7.8   FT.com's viral game
– The Wall Street Dash

Figure 7.9   FT.com's viral
game – Refer a Friend

per user session. Over a period of three weeks, over 28,000 users registered and played the game. The accompanying banner advertising also performed well, delivering good quality traffic to the site and resulting in over 50% of visitors playing the game, of which 29% returned three further times to play.

The campaign was also supported by HTML e-mail, which delivered a 10% response to the site and the viral nature of the campaign (users passing on the game, e-mail or web address to friends and colleagues) boosted user registrations by a further 18%.

5 KEY TIPS **Ensuring your viral campaign is successful**

1. **Avoid gimmicks** and make the subject of the viral useful.

2. Where possible, **incentivize** the viral.

3. Keep your viral to as **small a file size** as possible.

4. Ensure it is **easy to pass on** by e-mail.

5. Make the viral **accessible**. Utilize e-mail and web sites as your distribution channels.

7.3 Banner advertising and pop-ups

Banner ads are static or animated invitations to viewers to click on them and be 'jumped' to a destination page, commonly on the advertiser's web or micro site.

Recent research suggests that online advertising revenues are growing exponentially. There are three core types of online advertisement. Each one provides a direct link to a specific, targeted destination. They are:

1. Banner advertisements

The web's equivalent of TV commercials. More specifically, they are rectangular graphics (468 × 60 pixels typically) that are static, animated or rich-media in form. Banners typically link back to the advertiser's web site.

2. Sponsorship

When an advertiser sponsors an entire web site or section of a web site a sponsorship deals may include banner ads, prominent logo placements, exclusives, content and promotions. In most cases, sponsorship allows for a direct link to the sponsor's web site.

3. Interstitials

These are ads that open a second browser window. Commonly referred to as "Pop-ups", they appear as static ads or 15-30 second multimedia commercials. Interstitials can also be used for customer research, such as surveys or running promotions, to communicate a detailed message.

Since their development five years ago, banners continue to be used widely as a form of web advertising and comprise the majority of all ads online. Sponsorship accounts for 29%, and interstitials make up 6%.

BEST PRACTICE EMARKETING

There are currently three main types of banner ads:

- **Static banners** – display a constant, unchanging message.
- **Animated banners** – contain flashing or moving elements. Their animation is often generated through the use of a series of layers using animated GIF technology, such as Java.
- **Rich-media banners** – described in greater detail below.

Despite continuing popularity, average click-through rates for typical banners have fallen to less than 0.05%. Advertisers are increasingly turning to 'rich-media' – a technology that allows Flash, video and audio interaction, as well print capabilities within the banner. Studies suggest that rich media banners lead to higher brand awareness and improved response levels. Rich-media banners often use streaming audio and video to offer higher interactivity. Rich-media technology, such as Macromedia's Flash, can capture transactions fully within the banner, allow users to play games, or communicate brand messages with sound and movement. Figures 7.10 and 7.11 are two examples of rich-media banners whose creative content capture the user's attention and supports the overall branding message. In the case of the Britannic Money pop-up, this was designed by shrinking earth and utilized the print capabilities of Flash 4, allowing users to interact with the advert and print information from it without visiting the main Britannic Money web site.

Figure 7.10   Product pop-up advertisement used by Britannic Money

Figure 7.11 shows a pop-up from online bank Cahoot. Here, Cahoot successfully used their pop-up to communicate the benefits of their newly launched mobile banking service. The pop-up not only acted as an advertisement, but also as a presentation or demonstration of the service. The call to action was for users to then register for the service – integrating data capture.

Figure 7.11   A Pop-up from online bank Cahoot

Figure 7.12   Lucozade banner ad featuring streaming video of Lara Croft

STRENGTHS

- Ability to reach a global audience of Internet users
- Targeting
- Brand Awareness
- Traffic Generation

WEAKNESSES

- Response rates (average 0.05%)
- Costs
- Interactivity limited by technology
- Banner burn-out – over-exposed form of advertising

Measuring banner advertising

Measuring banners has largely been unreliable. Part of the problem is that marketers lacked an appropriate measurement tool and reporting standards, making comparing and contrasting potential ad buys difficult or impossible. Tools, such as Netgenesis, I/Pro and NetCount all employ different standards and methodologies, thus generating uneven and inconsistent results. To combat this problem, CASIE (the Coalition for Advertising Supported Information & Entertainment) was established in 1997 and standardized online media measurement for more accurate results. This work was complemented with the advent of the FAST Forward interactive advertising body's sub-committee on creating voluntary measurement standards.

Today, measurement tools like Nielsen Net/Ratings and Media Metrix are more advanced, albeit limited in their reach. However, as the industry matures, advertisers will increasingly demand in-depth reports and must have access to data that goes far beyond hits and click-throughs.

 Everybody in leather
www.gap.com

Figure 7.13   Banner ad for GAP

5 steps to developing a banner ad campaign

The key development elements of a banner campaign encompass planning, creative, production, execution and measurement. The process below briefly outlines these five steps, typically experienced when working with your advertising agency to produce an interactive advertising campaign, such as a banner campaign:

1. Planning

Planning the campaign starts with the brief which specifies the components of the campaign, including the target audience and related segmentation, business, marketing and communications objectives, and campaign positioning. It will then go on to describe the ad placements, desired site placements, campaign run (or flight), traffic goals and site requirements for banner sizes, types, etc.

2. Creative concepting

The concepting process is the development and review between you and your agency of creative comparisons, including banner mock-ups of copy and graphics. Your agency will typically present multiple mock-ups and variations. This is followed by discussion of rationale and approach, then sign-off of the preferred executions.

3. Production

Following the appropriate rounds of creative review, the approved concepts are produced as actual campaign 'assets' (these are the physical banners) with a final review before sending the banners to the media agency for placement on web sites according to the media plan.

4. Execution

Execution is when the banners are 'trafficked' or placed – the campaign assets are delivered to the site placements and tracked to ensure they achieve the metrics of the campaign to fulfil the media plan.

5. Measurement

Measurement is achieved by using 'click-counters' in the banners to report the number of times the banner has been served (impressions) and the number of times web users have seen the banner and clicked on it (click-throughs) jumping to the destination page that the banner points to. Through these figures we can then tell whether the campaign has been successful in achieving our desired metrics stated in the media plan.

The timescale for developing and implementing a banner campaign can be anything from an afternoon to several weeks, depending on the requirements of the plan. The approximate costs vary subject to the execution used. Banner ads produced as animated gifs are less expensive than rich-media banners using Flash, which take a greater amount of time to produce.

In order to plan and execute a successful online ad campaign, marketing professionals should consider:

- Careful media planning and integration – define clear commercial objectives.

- Use cross-media advertising – utilize a mix of media channels to deliver the message to the target audience.

There are a wide variety of banner advertising sizes and specifications. The Interactive Advertising Bureau has recently announced (10th April 2001) several new sizes of banners ads. Information about banner advertising can be found at the IAB's web site, www.iab.net.

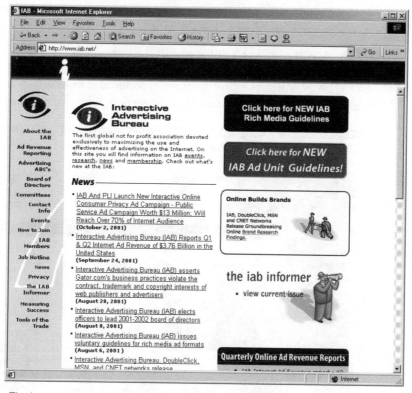

Figure 7.14   The Interactive Advertising Bureau's web site

7.4 Micro sites

A micro site is a small web site that may or may not be 'inside' a larger web site and is generally comprised of only a few web pages. Typically, it is designed to focus on a specific message (or brand), sponsorship or offer. For example, a company may run a promotion and create a micro site to support it. When the promotion is over, the micro site is taken down and any links to it are removed from the linked site(s).

Think of a micro site as a cut-down version of a web site, developed specifically to promote a brand, product or campaign. Micro sites are an effective method of marketing for many companies in the B2B and B2C sectors. They can offer brand awareness in the digital marketplace and provide a platform for driving traffic to the main web site, call centre or even facilitating research, as well as enticing visitors to purchase products or services.

A micro site can be very handy, because:

1. It allows for a short, memorable domain name all of its own (because it doesn't have to be buried within the hierarchy of a larger site);

2. It doesn't require extensive navigational changes to an existing site, since it exists separately to support a specific message or campaign and only a few pages in the entire site link to it;

3. It's easy to take down at the end of the promotion/campaign.

Diesel's 'Daily African Online' micro site, pictured in Figure 7.15, is a satirical look at the world as if Africa were the leading nation, not a third world country.

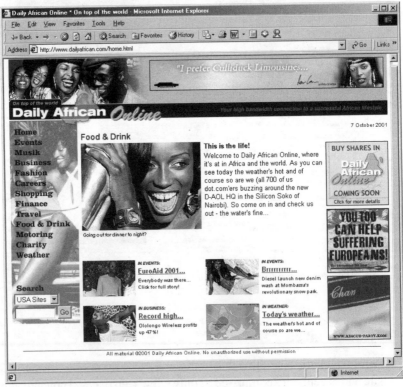

Figure 7.15   Diesel's Daily African Online micro site

British Airway's 21ˢᵗ Century Air Travel micro site is designed to promote the benefits of their World Traveller packages through the use of rich-media content that the user can interact with, giving an enhanced experience of the brand and promoting the values of the service being offered.

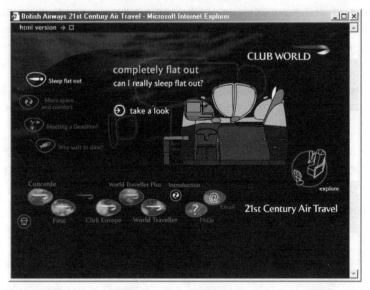

Figure 7.16   British Airway's 21ˢᵗ Century Air Travel micro site

STRENGTHS

- Extends your market reach to a global audience of Internet users
- Can be deployed across your own site or other companies
- Campaign specific 'add-on' that sits outside your main web site
- Offers interaction for marketing, branding and selling products
- Adds value to the communications and sales cycles
- Enhances the company/brand/product awareness

WEAKNESSES

- Need to be dynamic to be compelling
- Web is over-crowded
- Interactivity is limited by technology
- Need to be maintained
- Can be costly to deploy

BEST PRACTICE EMARKETING

7.5 Content and the multi-channel marketing environment

e-Marketing and e-business are leading to the emergence of a multi-channel culture, driven by technology that is enabling people to access content from a range of different devices. The ongoing development of multi-channel marketing will give rise to a need to re-purpose content for devices that offer 'moment-driven' access. Your customers will use more devices for more and more 'moments of interactivity' with your brand.

Content will no longer be associated with a particular media type, but all media types. Therefore, your content has to be designed for all media types.

Content re-purposing is the adaptation of some piece of data for a new purpose. That means transferring it from one format or type, to another so that it may be displayed on a different device or platform.

USEFUL WEB SITES	Purposing content for different channels
Content Rules	www.contentt-rules.com/eprise/main/contentrules
Ntl	www.ntl.co.uk
Open	www.open-here.co.uk
W3C Org	www.w3.org/People/Bos/DesignGuide/repurposing.html

Re-purposing web content for WAP

WAP may be big, but a quarter of web sites that have been re-purposed for WAP don't work! This was the key finding of a new report from WAP development portal www.anywhereyougo.com. One in four WAP sites are riddled with faults making them inaccessible to users, says the report, and it's all because of a few simple errors in the coding of WML (Wireless Mark-up Language) pages that are causing the problem. Around 28% of the 50 sites tested by AnyWhereYouGo.com are said to have contained damaging errors. Part of the problem with WAP sites currently is that marketers often fail to take into account the current limitations of today's mobile devices. Most WAP sites seem to be uploaded straight from web sites and therefore the text used is sometimes too long, links are broken or the information is un-navigable on a WAP browser.

Today WAP designers are designing for multiple devices, each requiring different coding, making development more complex and expensive than simply designing for conventional web browsers.

KEY TIPS FOR RE-PURPOSING CONTENT FOR WAP

- Stick to one mobile device until the technology catches up

- Investigate programming languages such as XML (eXtensible Markup Language) that can automatically   render WAP content for different handsets

- Investigate more complex 'Middleware' that delivers content to the WAP-browser regardless of the network provider, screen size, device type and information being shown.

Middleware is the 'glue' or a layer of software between a network and the applications it runs. This provides services such as identification, authentication, authorization, directories and security.

Re-purposing web content for iTV

Interactive TV is a rich new media platform that converges the best of TV, the PC, and Internet. iTV offers ease of use through a remote control; the modular scalability of the PC and the interactivity of the web. The convergence of the television set and the Internet offers many exciting possibilities for the marketer but also many challenges to transfer content across. Internet content needs to be re-purposed for television. You can't read it unless you're practically on top of the set! The problem is, there are now five different types of iTV offering in the UK alone, each based on different technology making, content re-purposing highly complicated.

6 key steps for re-purposing content for iTV

1. Create new HTML content (or clean up existing pages)
2. Remove all links and banner ads relating to the Internet
3. Reduce 'screen clutter' that is inappropriate to iTV
4. Increase font sizes to make text easy to read
5. Review line thicknesses and colours used
6. Seek technical information on buttons, icons, screen templates and linking applications such as e-mail, chat, reminders and payment gateways.

But what if you don't want to do the re-purposing yourself? A whole range of companies exist that offer tools that will automatically clean up web pages for interactive TV.

4 steps to strategic content re-purposing

1. Think 'transmedia'

- Give up the old model of creating content solely for the web and then trying to re-purpose it for other media like mobile devices or iTV.

- Move your content, branding and marketing across multiple platforms.

- Develop materials that can be selected and arranged to produce many different forms.

Transmedia is the ability to operate across multiple, different communications channels each having their own specific methods of delivering content to the receiving difference.

2. Create environments

- Focus not on the message solely, but on the environment

- Use channels that will support many messages, brands and offers.

- Obey the physical laws of the channel, such as limited data speeds, screen sizes, viewing distances and font sizes, without losing creativity.

3. Invite your audience to become authors

- Engage your target audience in your content development

- Seek user insight into what works, what doesn't and what is meaningful or just marketing experimentation.

- Test, test and test again until it is right for the end-user.

4. Create scenarios for various devices and contexts

- Test your content's resilience across different platforms and through different devices. In other words, be sure that you have created material that can be supported by a diverse range of media types.

Thinking transmedia means planning for producing your content across multiple digital channels, outside of the PC environment. Most other devices have lower screen resolutions, are viewed from a greater distance and have a different style of navigation to the Internet, so that content developed for web sites will not work except on a computer..

USEFUL WEB SITES **Referenced in this chapter**

Forrester Research	www.forrester.com
Oasis Communications	www.oasis.com
eMarketer	www.emarketer.com
Tony Stone	www.tonystone.com
Joe Cartoon	www.joecartoon.com
FT.com	www.ft.com
Macromedia	www.macromedia.com
Interactive Advertising Bureau	www.iab.net
Britannic Money	www.britannicmoney.com
British Airways	www.britishairways.com
Diesel's Daily African Online	www.dialyafrican.com

CHAPTER SUMMARY

In this chapter you have learnt that achieving best practice in e-marketing comprises:

- Understanding your customers' needs and the demands of your markets

- Integrating data capture of customer information into all marketing processes

- Focusing on your objectives that seek to close the gap between customer expectation and business deliverables

- Focusing on supporting the complete customer service cycle to ensure high Quality of Customer Experience

- Customizing messages where possible by tailoring products and services

- Integrating online marketing processes with offline processes to ensure seamless communications across the complete mix

- Using customer data to enhance the online experience, but enable customers to opt-out if they wish

- Sharing data with your customers by enabling them to have access to the business

- Integrating online loyalty programmes to drive customer buying to the web – this will reduce costs and enhance profitability

- Ensuring your online brand and offline brand messages and values are consistent.

TEST YOURSELF

1. One reason that e-mail marketing is such a strong and effective tool is that e-mail significantly outperforms traditional direct mail in response and conversion rates. *True or false?*

2. An e-mail campaign contributes to an integrated marketing strategy because it can perform the essential functions of several traditional marketing channels. *True or false?*

3. Developing an Opt-in mailing list from web site visitors is popular among marketers because it not only increases the opportunity to distribute e-mail newsletters but also leads to an increase in the cost of advertising for the newsletter's sponsorships. *True or false?*

4. Planning, developing and executing an e-mail marketing campaign takes less time than a direct mail campaign, and a majority of the responses can be expected within two weeks. *True or false?*

5. e-Mail marketing messages typically generate click-through-rates of 10-20%, which is higher than most direct mail campaigns and Web banner advertisements. *True or false?*

Chapter **8**

Best practice customer service online

OVERVIEW

This chapter introduces you to some important techniques your e-business can employ to ensure customer service levels stay high. We will look at key steps you can take to develop and implement your e-business customer service plan, as well as learn from other e-businesses that have successfully achieved high levels of customer service online.

LEARNING OBJECTIVES

In this chapter you will learn:

- How to develop a strategy for online customer service

- The principles of online customer service and techniques used

- How you can develop your customer service strategy

Chapter Topic	Specific Learning Objective
8.1 Customer Service Strategies	Considerations you should make for disaster recovery in e-business
8.2 Key priorities for Best Practice eCustomer Service	5 key steps to online service success
8.3 Developing your eCustomer Service Strategy	2 key initiatives to planning your service strategy and 7 key tips on winning and keeping online customers

KEYWORDS

Offer to Treat	Instant messaging	Co-browsing	eCRM
Digital ID	Electronic wallet	Encryption	

Notepad exercises: 1

8.0 Introduction

In e-business, customer service is king. Without appropriate customer service strategies being implemented, your e-business will not succeed! There are millions of sites on the World Wide Web today. Each and every one of these sites is different; they offer different things, in different ways by different companies. But there seems to be one thing that inextricably links many of today's e-businesses – poor customer service.

In e-business, customer service is king

Take this familiar story. Has it ever happened to you? A web user in the UK signs up with a US-based travel portal offering discounted deals on holidays and flights. The site requires the user to register and takes a one-time fee of $60 for providing access to the service. Having spent time registering, which in this case was an over-complicated and labour-intensive process, the user is then asked to complete the process by entering their credit card details. Having done all this and having spent over five minutes creating an account, the customer is then told that they must ring a local number in the USA. Is this good customer service? No! What's more, that potential customer, and ten others may then be lost.

Recent research from DataMonitor says that 7.8 per cent of abandoned sales over the Internet could have been saved and converted. In the global e-business economy, this loss accounts for as much as $6.1bn in lost sales in 1999 alone. If the trend were to continue, it could represent as much as $173bn in salvageable sales over the next five years. Meanwhile, the average e-business with a customer service strategy in place could have improved its sales by 35 per cent in 2000. Frightening stuff. What's more alarming is that in their rush to establish an e-business presence, most have forgotten or neglected the basic proposition of customer service until it's too late. It seems that much higher on the check-list is urgency to establish the online brand, whilst more fundamental issues like good customer service, site usability and so on fall by the wayside.

There are many examples of e-businesses that establish themselves too quickly and give too little thought to customer service issues. One such example is failed fashion retailer boo.com (which we look at in more detail later in the case studies in Chapter 11). The site suffered from all sorts of customer service issues, starting with its very own interactive sales assistant, Miss Boo, through to poor delivery of content to the user's browser and its inability to physically deliver on time the goods customers had ordered.

8.1 Customer service strategies

Customer service can be split into two areas. Firstly, it's about getting the delivery of your online proposition right every time, consistently providing a functional, high quality of customer experience (QofCE) within your site, as discussed earlier in Chapter 6, through to ensuring you deliver the right product to the right person within the right timescale and to the right address. The second and slightly more reactive type of good customer service strategy is disaster recovery. What do you do and how quickly can you do it if something in your e-business goes wrong?

A clear example of poor disaster recovery was demonstrated when the online business of UK-based high street catalogue merchant Argos mistakenly placed a 21" Sony Trinitron Television set for sale on its web site at the price of £2.99 instead of £299.00. This is what's known as an 'offer to treat', which means that while Argos offered the TV set for sale at that price, it did not have to sell the product at that price. Many opportunistic buyers took advantage of Argos's mistake and placed orders via their credit card. However, even though Argos accepted the orders and provided customers with a unique order reference, thereby establishing a contract, it was 'subject to availability'! Needless to say, they did not honour the orders and left many customers with a bitter e-business taste in their mouth. At the same time, they offered the great British press an excellent story that was quickly followed by an onslaught of criticism from the public and the e-business industry.

The moral of the story is this. If you don't get your systems, procedures and most importantly your customer services right, customers will stop buying from you. Argos learned some valuable lessons from this, including content management, but they also quickly understood the meaning of disaster recovery and crisis management.

On the other hand, let's look at an e-business that is getting it right. Frequently referenced, Amazon.com is one of the first e-businesses to master customer service. They have got it right and they did from the very beginning of their existence. Amazon illustrates that good customer service is the key to gaining and retaining customers (see Figure 8.2).

For Amazon, good customer service is offset with being one of the more expensive booksellers on the Internet. BOL and WHSmith Online both offer larger discounts, but customers continue to buy from Amazon because it makes the purchasing process easy and the after-sales service is consistently excellent.

A good e-business needs to be upfront about things like inventory levels and post and packaging costs before the sale is made. If it's not, it will leave customers disappointed, angry and unwilling to use the site next time in favor of a competitor site that is more upfront. Good e-business requires accuracy

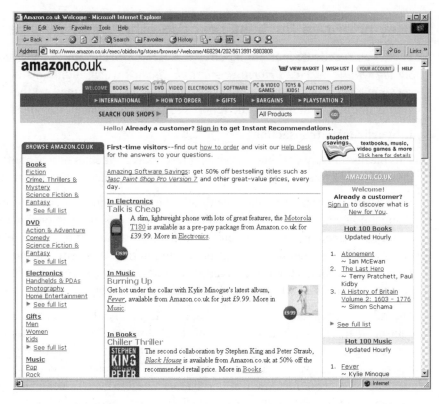

Figure 8.1   Amazon's UK web site

of information (take the Argos case), clarity of what's required from the customer in the transaction and an understanding of how much the transaction is going to cost. Other information, such as delivery timescales, after sales support and returns policies also need to be easily available to the customer.

This is good e-business practice in customer service and will ensure customers continue to have a high quality of experience with your brand.

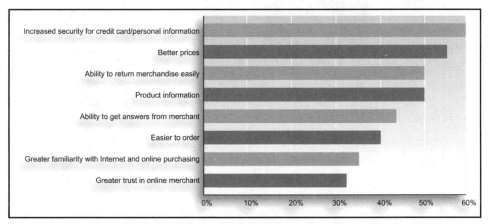

Figure 8.2   Consumers differentiate based on price and customer service

8.2 Key priorities for best practice eCustomer service

There's an excellent report from Forrester Research on customer service called *Setting Online Service Priorities: First, the Basics* which highlights the key, yet simple priorities that an e-business must address before they set their stall out for trading. In summary, the report suggests that e-businesses must:

1. Synchronize transactions

This means that any customer service representative, whether online or offline, should be able to see customer transactions that originate in any channel.

Take Sweden's largest bank, SwedBank. They have implemented a multi-channel e-business strategy that enables both business and personal banking customers 'freedom of movement' across all communications channels, to include the high street branch, telephone and Internet. A SwedBank customer can have an account enquiry resolved at any one of the bank's communications points, regardless of where their details sit within the organization.

The rules of engagement have changed. Traditionally, the brand has been in control of how it communicates with its customers. Now, the customer is controlling communication and choosing, if not dictating, how they wish to be communicated with, when and what's said. This relates directly to a key measure of success for how well (or badly) an e-business is achieving good customer service – does the customer discriminate between online channels and off? If they do, and favour online, then that represents a strong measure that the site is working well.

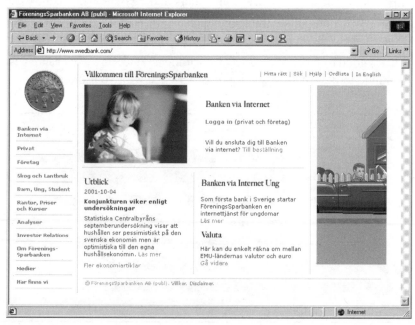

Figure 8.3 SwedBank's home page

2. Ensure e-mail works

e-mail is described as the Internet's killer application and one that can act as a primary service channel. A survey of the top 100 retail and financial sites in the UK, conducted by ServiceSoft, showed that 47 per cent of web sites did not respond to e-mail queries (see Table 8.1).

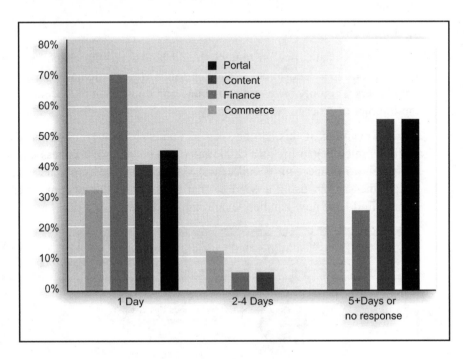

Table 8.1   *Response times vary from good to bad*

Forrester suggests that e-businesses must *'target an under four-hour response time, leverage the same knowledge base as phone agents and enable access across all channels as 40% of consumers use more than one channel.'* One important thing to bear in mind, however, is that a separate piece of research by the same company states that 41% of consumers prefer using the telephone for customer service enquiries.

40% of consumers use more than one channel... 41% prefer using the telephone

One UK company leveraging e-mail in a sophisticated manner is Barclays Bank. The bank responds to online queries with an automated e-mail acknowledging the request and suggesting that if the customer wants to be proactive rather than wait in a call centre queue, they can click on the link to the database that the call centre accesses and help themselves.

3. Identify profitable customers

Forrester further suggests that e-businesses must seek to identify their most profitable customers *'in order to prioritize resources when unpredictable service demands cause a backlog of calls.'* The report says that up to 57 per cent of companies are not currently aware of the identity of their most important customers.

4. Online customer services

Forrester also states that customers should be offered the chance to talk to someone online as a customer service option. This is particularly pertinent for home users who only have one phone line and don't want to disconnect from the Internet in order to resolve a query.

A good example of this can be seen at Lands' End, the US casual clothes retailer, which began life as a catalogue company. This e-business enables it customers to connect to its call centre via the web site by phone, e-mail or instant-messaging, using a window that pops up on the customer's screen. Lands' End Live now handles several hundred messages a day.

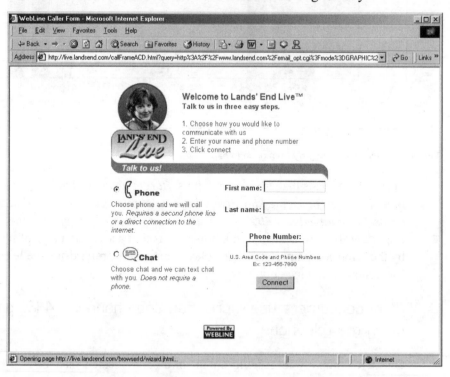

Figure 8.4   Lands' End Live – Connecting customers to their call centre

Figure 8.5   Lands' End Live –
Instant Messaging service

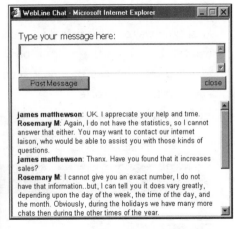

Figure 8.6   Lands' End WebLine Chat Live

5.   Co-browsing

Forrester's final suggestion is co-browsing – this can be useful for customers where there are particularly complicated products, such as financial services, cars and computers. Co-browsing enables the customer and the sales representative to share views of the web page. Cisco Systems estimate that this technology can help e-businesses reduce abandonment of shopping baskets for complex products by 66 per cent.

Co-browsing is one of the technologies we discuss in Chapter 9, when reviewing best practice electronic Customer Relationship Management (eCRM).

CASE STUDY: RS Components

One of the best examples of effective customer service within the B2B sector can be found within the £8bn global market for electronic and mechanical component products. UK-based RS Components' e-business handles over 300,000 different products. Customers can place their orders via a call centre, having consulted the RS Components catalogue, or online via the web site and be assured of 99% availability on all products carried, as well as guaranteed next day delivery for items ordered up to 8.00p.m. that day.

In addition, 300,000 customers who have accounts set-up with RS via the web site can access their previous trading details with RS as far back as thirteen months and receive personalized, specific shopping areas based on their pre-defined purchasing profile.

Last year, RS Components launched a new broadvision-powered site. First-time visitors are asked to register and complete a profile which is used to customize the content on the customers own 'home page', enabling them to see the most recent offers on products that match specifically their profile.

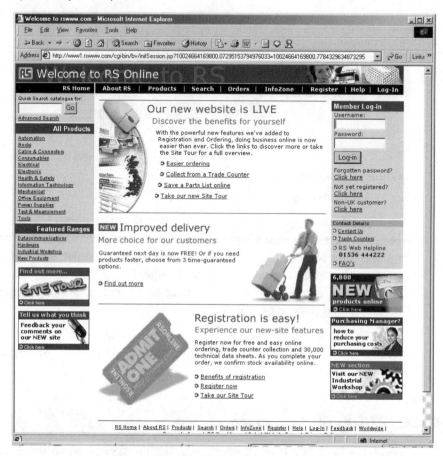

Figure 8.7   The RS Components Internet Channel

NOTEPAD EXERCISE

As a budding e-business entrepreneur, place yourself in the shoes of your customer. For many customers, if they have a question, they will seek to have it answered either face to face by a member of the brand's staff within a shop or office, or over the phone via a call centre. The equivalent requirement exists online. Write down five key ways in which you can deliver customer service via the web.

The global state of customer service

Currently, customer service in the US is ahead of the European market, according to recent research conducted by Jupiter. Their report shows that 46% of US sites contacted during the study took five or more days to respond to e-mail enquiries, while some never responded at all. In Europe, sites had an even worse record, with 56% in the same category (see Table 8.1).

8.3 Developing your eCustomer service strategy

If the examples of Amazon and RS don't inspire you enough, here's a simple checklist that you can follow as part of your e-business strategy planning phase. But remember, achieving best practice in customer service on the Internet and through other digital channels requires skill in many areas, including online support, security, accessibility, fulfilment and more.

Step 1: Promote comfort

While e-business continues to gain mass acceptance amongst businesses and consumers, security of the Internet, web and digital channels generally remains one issue that stands in the way of global customer acceptance. For e-business to achieve, and indeed exceed project revenues, buyers and sellers will need to have complete confidence in the privacy and security of the data they transmit and store.

It is the role of every responsible e-business company to ensure that they communicate and promote confidence for trading online. The Interactive Media in Retail Group (IMRG) has established a useful code of practice for companies wishing to set-up business on the web. The full code of practice can be seen at www.imrg.org/hallmark/default.htm. This means that e-businesses displaying the Hallmark have adhered to the code of practice and implemented stringent controls to ensure they achieve best practice.

Figure 8.8   The IMRG Hallmark

Providing a high quality of customer experience can be achieved relatively easily. By following the models set-out by Amazon and RS, you can enable your customers to have access to their information online anytime, anywhere, through a simple but secure account facility. This empowers your customer to use their profile in a way that is meaningful and valuable to them. For example, they can check their account status; where their current order is in the system and their order history.

Another way to promote confidence and offer service is to use a secure Internet technology such as digital IDs and electronic wallets, e.g. Microsoft Passport.

British Telecom launched Trustwise (www.trustwise.com), a digital certificate service aimed at enhancing the security of e-businesses by guaranteeing secure communication between the site and its customers. The Trustwise service offers digital IDs (or certificates) for entire web sites or personal IDs for the encryption of individual users' e-mail.

An alternative method is SET (Secure Electronic Transactions) developed by MasterCard and Visa (www.setco.org). SET, which was established in February 1996 as a joint venture between MasterCard and Visa International, uses a system of locks and keys along with a certified account ID for both consumers and e-business businesses. Through a unique process of 'encrypting' or scrambling the information exchanged between the customer and the e-business site, SET ensures a payment process that is convenient, private and most of all secure. Specifically, SET has sought to:

1. Establish an industry standard to keep customer data, orders and payment information confidential.

2. Increase the integrity of all transmitted data on the Net through encryption.

3. Provide authentication to the business that a cardholder is a legitimate user of a branded payment/credit card account.

4. Provide authentication that a company can accept branded payment card transactions through its relationship with an acquiring financial institution, such as NatWest Streamline or Barclays Merchant Services.

5. Allow the use of the best security practices and system design techniques to protect all legitimate parties in an e-business transaction.

e-business sites displaying the SET logo have met the above security criteria for transacting online.

Step 2: Deliver customer service and satisfaction to the door!

If you want to survive the e-economy, then your objective, over the long term, must be to retain profitable customers for longer. If that's your objective, then your strategy must be to achieve this by developing customer satisfaction in their experiences with your brand both on and offline. Delivering content-rich, interactive experiences begins to enhance relationships and provide customers with consistent, complete information. This in turn enables them to make better, quicker, more informed decisions about products and services that they want to buy.

But it doesn't stop there. Achieving long-term customer retention requires a long, hard look at our levels of service and support. You have already read how some brands enhance the customer experience by providing greater interactivity with the business (such as Lands' End), but that same level of interactivity should, therefore, be made available on policies and procedures, and staff who can answer specific questions asked by individual customers.

Four other key initiatives you could introduce to achieve best practice in online customer service are:

1. Provide a Returns Policy and Privacy Policy up-front.
2. Offer multiple points of contacts, such as Call Me buttons to the call centre, online chat, freefone numbers, mailing addresses, fax numbers and email addresses.
3. Offer free shipping.
4. Provide a returns address and mailing label with all products you ship.

Summary

Each of the examples illustrate that an e-business must not forget that age-old, basic business rules apply equally to new channels. Success, or lack of it, is often a result of forgetting such basic considerations. The National Opinion Poll predicted that online shopping in the UK will be worth £10bn during 2001, whilst in Europe 97 million Europeans are online generating £53bn in Internet sales and Forrester predict that US B2B and B2C eCommerce will reach $550bn. If this proves to be true, you will be well advised to invest in good customer service to ensure your customers keep coming back for more.

A GUIDE TO WINNING AND KEEPING ONLINE CUSTOMERS

1. Shoppers will browse many sites to compare costs. Be upfront about your prices, duty and shipping charges.

2. Referrals are a great source of new business offline. This applies equally online. Use web directories, search engines, affiliates programmes and strategic links to drive new traffic to your site. These sources of new business will be your cheapest.

3. Confirm any interactions with customers by e-mail, specifically for orders, queries and complaints.

4. Integrate all communications channels, to include mail order, the telephone, fax, mobile devices, iTV and so on.

5. If you are selling products that cost more than £100 per unit, offer money-back guarantees on credit card transactions and be prepared to remove concerns of fraud from the customer's mind.

6. Provide security and privacy throughout the online buying process by using data encryption and secure socket layers (secure servers).

7. If your goods cost less than £18.00 per unit, then offer shipping free of charge, anywhere in the world.

USEFUL WEB SITES	Referenced in this chapter
Argos	www.argos.co.uk
Amazon	www.amazon.com
SwedBank	www.swedbank.com
Barclays Bank	www.barclays.com
Lands' End	www.landsend.com
RS Components	www.rscomponents.com
IMRG	www.imrg.org
British Telecom TrustWise	www.trustwise.com
Secure Electronic Transactions (SET)	www.setco.org
Datamonitor	www.datamonitor.com
Jupiter	www.jupiter.com

CHAPTER SUMMARY

In this chapter, you have learnt:

1. That every e-business should always plan for a disaster. Remember Argos and Boo.com – don't be like them!

2. That effective customer service online is based around giving customers two things: 1. a choice of channels to use in order to talk to your customer service representatives; and 2. sufficient levels of information up front, so that they can make informed purchase decisions.

3. That achieving best practice in online customer service means your e-business will need to master many disciplines, including customer support, security, accessibility and fulfilment.

4. That winning and keeping customers online is about trust, integrity, advocacy and openness – employ these factors and not only will customers be loyal, but they will become your greatest source of new business.

TEST YOURSELF

1. Good customer service online is about delivering a consistently good experience each and every time and being able to meet the expectations you set. *True or false?*

2. It is acceptable that an e-business does not respond to inbound email enquiries from customers, as demonstrated by 47% of companies polled in the ServiceSoft research. *True or false?*

3. e-Businesses that offer customer service through multiple channels are more likely to be successful than those that do not offer the customer a choice. *True or false?*

4. SET stands for Synchronized e-business Testing and was developed to help e-business check whether they were offer good levels of customer service online. *True or false?*

5. By providing greater levels of interactivity, e-business can enhance the customer service experience. *True or false?*

Chapter 9

Online customer
relationship management

OVERVIEW

This chapter introduces eCRM, personalization and the e-business extranet. It explores the benefits of eCRM to e-businesses and how to develop a strategy for it. It also defines and reviews personalization – how to develop it within your e-business plan, the approach and technologies for delivering it and who's doing it. Finally, it introduces extranets – private, secure Internet-based trading and information environments used by businesses to engage customers and meet their specific needs.

LEARNING OBJECTIVES

In this first chapter you will learn about:

- eCRM, what it is and how to develop your strategy to include it
- Techniques YOU can use to capture customer data
- How to mine customer data for effective e-marketing
- Personalization techniques and technologies
- Extranets and their role in e-business

Chapter Topic	Specific Learning Objective
9.1 What is eCRM	To understand eCRM and its role in e-business
9.2 Building an eCRM strategy	To understand the three key steps in developing an eCRM strategy
9.3 Capturing customer data	How to use different methods of data capture to profile customers
9.4 Customer data analysis	How to analyse customer data gathered from multiple sources
9.5 Personalization	To understand personalization and its benefits
9.6 Effective eCRM	How to deliver best practice eCRM
9.7 Return on Investment	Understanding the cost implications of eCRM
9.8 Extending your net	To understand extranets and their role in e-business

KEYWORDS

eCRM	Data Warehouse	Return on Investment (ROI)
Cookies	Personalization	Collaborative Filtering
Online Surveys	Customer Profiling	Intelligent Call Routing (ICR)
Extranet	Auto-responder	Customer Service Representatives (CSR)

Notepad Exercises: 2

9.0 Introduction

The deployment of eCRM systems is aggressive. Businesses are rushing to implement e-Service solutions with little regard for customer requirements or return on investment (ROI). In this chapter, we shall explore exactly what eCRM is all about — how to implement it within the context of your business and your customers and how it works in relation to the call centre and other digital channels.

9.1 What is eCRM?

Before we talk about the 'how' to do eCRM, let's understand what it is. What is electronic Customer Relationship Management?

eCRM is the process of increasing customer retention through improved satisfaction. eCRM stands for electronic Customer Relationship Management - a series of coordinated steps that are designed to boost sales revenue and strengthen the interactive relationship that exists between you and your customer.

This improved relationship is achieved by focusing on your most valuable customers and tailoring your products, services and communications to their individual preferences.

CRM recognises that a company is more likely to profit from cultivating existing customers than from continuously investing in new business and then making no effort to retain it. When Advertising Age asked the Direct Marketing Association President H. Robert Wientzen about eCRM, he compared it to high school sex:

"Everybody talks about it. Everybody thinks everybody else is doing it, and those that are doing it are doing it badly."
H Robert Wientzen, 16 April, 2001

It is suggested that the integration of eCRM into your e-business strategy is known to:

- Reduce customer attrition by 10 per cent;
- Increase profitability by 20 per cent;
- Achieve a Return-On-Investment (ROI) within six months of implementation.

So what does eCRM offer? eCRM seeks to address a number of critical business problems, to include:

- Loss of competitive advantage
- Customer attrition to competitors
- Cost control of customer relationships
- Poor response rates to marketing communications and promotions
- Poor or falling sales
- Inadequate knowledge and understanding of customer needs.

eCRM is a powerful strategy that can be used to solve business problems and meet strategic objectives. These objectives include:

- Improving customer service
- Reducing business costs
- Increasing profitability
- Meeting increased global competition
- Responding faster to competitive challenges
- Providing transparent access to data
- Supporting faster, more informed decision-making processes.

9.2 Building your eCRM strategy

There are three simple processes to eCRM that will ensure your communications are relevant, timely and coordinated across on and offline channels, whilst also ensuring you are following the best practice guidelines highlighted earlier in relation to customer privacy, permission and data protection. The processes you need to follow to build a successful eCRM strategy are these.

Step 1: Identify your most profitable customers

For any company, simply knowing 'who buys what' is not sufficient to enable marketers to develop successful, profitable marketing campaigns. You need to know:

- Who your customers are, what they buy, their needs and expectations;
- How much you should invest in them;
- When you should contact them;
- Through which channel do they want the contact to take place;
- What levels of contact permission exist;
- What you should say to engage them in interaction.

An eCRM solution enables you to assess the lifetime value and the potential lifetime value of your customer relationships, and to determine the appropriate investment required for specific customer segments and individuals.

eCRM solutions are based on centralized data warehouses that provide detailed, unified customer information required for creating and executing effective communications and promotions strategies. eCRM allows you to identify your most profitable customers, quickly and efficiently.

> **Tip**: A data warehouse is a structure for organizing information systems using all possible data available in the enterprise to create one integrated view of the entire business. Typically, data warehouse systems consist of a set of programs that extract data from the operational environment, a database that maintains data, and systems that provide data to users.

Step 2: Personalize your communications by harnessing technology

In today's e-business world, the shift of power has moved to the customer and consumer. They are now in control. It is the end customer who dictates how, when and through what channels you communicate with them. The old rules of direct marketing no longer exist in this wired world.

Developing a personal dialogue with your customer is now more critical than ever. But in doing so, you must ensure you are able to abide by your customers' right to 'Opt-in' and 'Opt-out' of the communications cycle – you must respect their privacy and their rights. eCRM can:

- Help you build permission-based customer databases;
- Identify customers' preferences for communications content, frequency and channel delivery;
- Execute communications, maximize response rates and return on investment;
- Build goodwill among customers and prospects.

Step 3: Evaluate the results of your strategies

Once you've invested in eCRM, you need to be able to evaluate the results of your venture. Evaluation of eCRM effectiveness should include:

- Actual results vs projected outcomes;
- Changes in customer behaviour to particular communications;
- Assess effectiveness of subsequent customer interactions to enhancing the customer relationship.

ONLINE CUSTOMER RELATIONSHIP MANAGEMENT

THE BENEFITS OF eCRM TO YOUR CUSTOMERS

- Improved response time to requests for information

- Reduced costs of buying the product/service

- Reduced costs of using the product/service

- Immediate access to order status and information

- Greater breadth of solution options

- More responsive technical support.

As the costs of your system will most likely be passed onto customers, are these benefits enough and will they be prepared to pay for them?

NOTEPAD EXERCISE

Jot down a few thoughts on your customers. What kind of content or services do you think they will pay for from your e-business site?

Figure 9.1   The FT's web site at www.ft.com

Some argue that the customer will pay for an 'enhanced relationship', whilst others say that it is a myth that customers want and are prepared to pay for information-intensive 'personal' relationships. An example of an industry sector that has turned to a subscription model for information-rich content in the news publishing industry. Major brands, such as the Wall Street Journal and Financial Times have now restricted access to their content and implemented a fee structure for full access. Pressure from their offline presence has driven them to introduce the new model.

9.3 Capturing customer data for eCRM

Information is power, and, often the key to business success. Today, a business needs all sorts of marketing-driven information to improve its chances of success and the marketer's ability to make appropriate decisions about customers' needs and wants. Through eCRM, an e-business web site can capture live, up-to-date information from customers by asking them questions on an ad-hoc basis. For example, pop-ups can be triggered that ask customers to state their opinions or thoughts on certain topics or issues. By combining a mix of activities, data can be effectively gathered and analysed, providing a platform for better marketing and a better web presence that meets the needs of the target audience specifically.

Registration/purchase forms

Perhaps the most effective method of capturing customer data is through order and registration forms. Registration forms enable customers to interact with your web site by using question prompts about products, services, needs, wants and so on. Forms are a highly effective method of gathering data about customers that can be analysed and profiled as part of an ongoing eCRM programme that integrates loyalty. The key to successful data capture is to ensure that the customer's flow or thought processes are not interrupted by complex data entry or confusing navigation and that the process of registration is in some way incentivized, such as offering a discount on the first purchase or providing tailored content via e-mail or SMS alerts that meet the customers' profiled interests.

Customer surveys – market research

A good example of using online customer surveys was performed by www.nature.com, the online publishing arm of scientific magazine Nature. They have produced eight different customer satisfaction surveys on the Internet, designed to find out how well or badly they are doing. The survey is conducted by invitation and involves around two thousand subscribers to the journal. As data is captured from the survey, it is fed, real-time, into an online database, enabling nature.com to track customer responses and react to key patterns emerging as the survey takes place, rather than waiting until it is complete to review the results. Not only is this form of customer research extremely dynamic, but it is also highly cost-effective, as the invitation to participate was issued by e-mail and the survey served many users at one time. In total, this form of customer research and data capture cost Nature Publishing less than $1000.00.

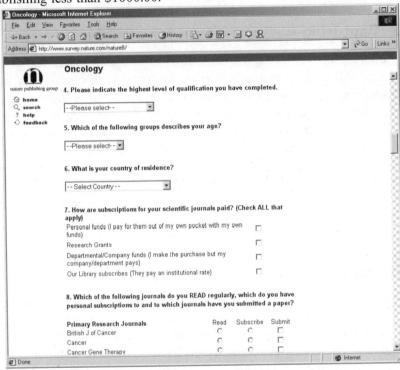

Figure 9.2   An online customer survey conducted by nature.com

Having collected customer data via registration forms or order forms, beware of the phenomenon known as 'stateless communication'. This occurs widely on the Internet and typically with large e-business sites that have not integrated their data capture and customer databases properly.

Tip: Stateless communication occurs when a customer registers for information or a service and returns at a later point to either request further information or purchase. On returning the site, stateless communication takes place when the site requires the already registered customer to re-enter their details, instead of pre-populating the form with existing information. The use of cookies or providing customers with a user ID are two simple steps for overcoming this.

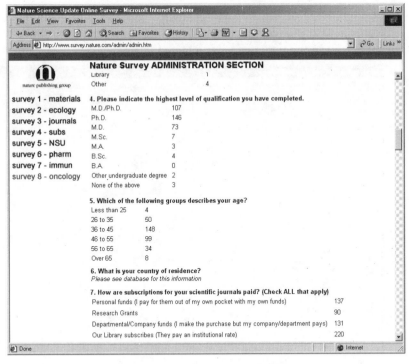

Figure 9.3   *The online results database of the survey, collated in real-time*

Online focus groups

Online focus groups are commonly held in Internet chat rooms, conducted using a moderator who will prompt questions and stimulate dialogue regarding a particular product, service or issue.

> **Tip**: A chat room is an area on the Internet where people can exchange information on any number of subjects. The chat room can enable communications either on a 1-to-1 basis or 1-to-many, and unlike e-mail, the process takes place in real-time, or with virtually no delay. Moderated chat rooms are where material submitted is monitored and unsuitable content removed before being made available to users.

A good example of using an online focus group is from leading financial services lender First Active Financial, who conducted their research with a group of ten independent financial advisors. The objective of the research was to find out more about this customer group's needs from their web site and understand better how they use the site so that First Active could develop it more specifically in the future. The research group was invited to participate in a series of online question and answer sessions, where they could contribute their thoughts about specific issues online and in real-time. The data was then analysed for common themes, and key learnings were actioned within future developments of the web site. Like the surveys, this method of customer research also proved very cost-effective and once set up, proved to be self-sustaining in the way users participated.

Figure 9.4   Online Focus Group research conducted by First Active Financial

Cookies

When a visitor enters the Home Page of your e-business site or a page within the site, the server on which your site resides can place a 'cookie' – a small string of numbers and letters – on to the visitor's computer. This small file of information can provide the e-business marketer with a tracking aid that can facilitate future actions during that visitor's session within your site.

A *cookie* is a text-only string of alphanumeric characters that gets entered into the memory of a browser. This string contains the domain, path, lifetime and value of a variable that a web site sets. If the lifetime of this variable is longer than the time the user spends at that site, then this string is saved to file for future reference.

Cookies require no direct interaction as such with the user, but allow the e-business marketer to identify different aspects of how the visitor uses the site.

For example, cookies can provide us with the following information:

- How the visitor navigates the web site – pages visited
- The point of entry into the site and the point of exit
- Products selected and placed within the shopping basket, but not purchased during that session
- The visitor's name and e-mail address – this can be used for basic personalization
- Which advertising or promotional mechanics the visitor has seen

Cookies can be a valuable source of customer data, as they enable the e-business site owner to monitor how potential customers and existing customers use the web site; how they search using keywords; how they navigate the site and which products they select for purchase. Cookies can also provide useful, basic personalization. By collecting a visitor's name (and e-mail address, if desired) the site can then greet the visitor in a personal fashion – for example "Welcome James", the next time they visit, or by placing the contents of the shopping basket into the cookie, the next time the visitor returns to the site, the site can pre-populate the visitor's previous selections into the basket, directly from the cookie. Cookies, if used appropriately, can benefit and enrich the users' experience of your web site. However, some concerns do exist over cookies being an invasion of customer privacy, so if you are using them within your e-business site, be upfront and tell customers.

Figure 9.5   Cookies in the Temporary Internet Files folder of my PC

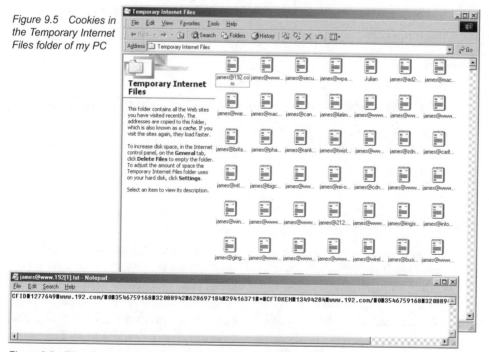

Figure 9.6   The contents of a cookie placed by American Express

9.4 Customer data analysis

Customer data is one of the most important assets any business has. That's why, as part of your eCRM strategy, good data analysis is essential. There are various techniques and processes involved in data analysis. The first is data collection, as discussed above, followed by the ability to analyse the data and then distribute it to the right people within the organization, where it can be put to best use, such as sales, marketing and customer services.

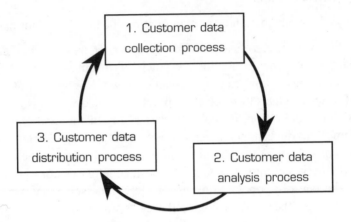

Figure 9.7 The Customer Data Cycle

To effectively mine data, you should look for key pointers such as:

- Customer usage patterns – frequency of visits; frequency/recency of purchases etc.?

- Purchase history – what did they purchase; when; size?

- Sales leads – what opportunities exist to up-sell; cross-sell; convert?

This data, taken from the customer database, should also be coupled to other data being generated by your online channels, such as server log files and site statistics.

9.5 Personalization

In the digital world as well as the physical, relationships evolve and grow through trust, responsiveness, and the mutual exchange of value. At a time when as many as 50 percent of visitors (your potential customers) abandon sites that require them explicitly to register, successful e-businesses should concentrate on the benefits of introducing true customer personalization, that allows them to effectively acquire new customers, build loyalty over time, and maximize the lifetime value of every customer and business partner.

Personalization is the combined use of technology and information to tailor e-commerce interactions between a business and individual customers. Using information previously obtained or provided in real-time about these and other customers, the exchange between the parties is altered to fit the customers' needs so that the transaction takes less time and delivers a product best suited to them.

Personalization – the beginnings of relationship commerce?

Delivering content, products or services and pricing specific to a unique customer's interests and needs is another tool we can use within the e-business environment. By collecting information about individual customer preferences, interests, and buying behaviour, we can target our offer more accurately, serving up information that is more likely to result in business transactions being made online. There are a variety of techniques, at a simple level, that we can use, including cookies and shopping histories. These enable our e-business database to remember every single customer that has ever visited our site and keep a detailed list of every item viewed or purchased. This, in turn, enables us to present new and related items to that customer based on what we know precisely matches their tastes and preferences.

Built-in intelligence in e-business sites also allows us to track how a customer searches and browses the site's pages, enabling this data to use pop-up special offers that match a pattern. For example, if the software identifies that a customer has browsed the same product more than once during the last seven days, we can assume that the customer is likely to buy, thereby delivering a pop-up content window with a message stating 'today only special – discount on X'. Additionally, we can also create product associations and present offers that state '10 free tennis balls with every racket purchased – today only'.

CASE STUDY: CAREERJOURNAL.COM

A good example of personalization is CareerJournal.com, a recruitment site from the Wall Street Journal. After users have completed a profiling questionnaire comprising of approximately ten questions, the site delivers relevant information against the data supplied. Within my personalized environment, careerjournal.com provides me with the latest news and features that are of relevance, together with the top job postings based on my specified job interests, by type and location. The site also delivers information on the latest salaries being paid in my area of specialization, as well as e-mail alerts of news and information relevant to my profile, delivered as either HTML or plain-text e-mail.

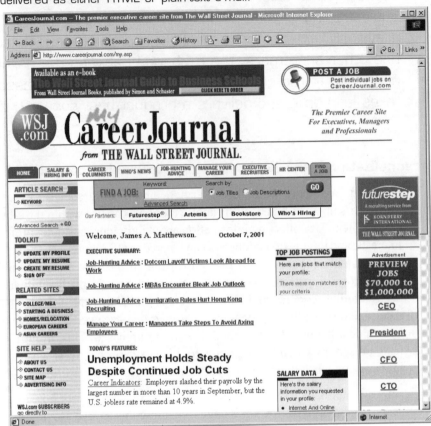

Figure 9.8   careerjournal.com from the Wall Street Journal using personalization

The advantages of personalization

Personalization enables an e-business to tailor ecommerce interactions to each individual customer. The purpose of this integration of technology with marketing is to deliver to the e-business and the customer the following benefits:

- Higher degrees of customer service to the customer by anticipating their needs and delivering content, products, services or pricing information that meets those needs;

- Enhancing the experience had by the customer, thereby increasing customer satisfaction levels;

- Improving the efficiency of the interaction and thereby increasing the likelihood of a purchase being made during that visit;

- Increasing the level of knowledge about customers and understanding why and how they prefer to do business with your organization;

- Building a relationship that encourages customer loyalty and increased customer value to the e-business, through subsequent purchases;

- Improving the performance of your e-business site by using tracking to provide your e-business with knowledge on what works and what doesn't. Personalization can help you to find out what makes your customer 'click'.

Personalization technologies

In e-business, there are two primary technologies used for online personalization: *collaborative filtering* and *customer profiling*.

Collaborative filtering allows a business to utilise the eCommerce experiences of a customer, or other customers that share a similar profile, to shape its electronic responses to each individual customer. Through the use of algorithms or equations, together with sophisticated data analysis, the history of past interactions produces a projection of a customer's future buying behaviour. This enables the business to offer a unique product or service for each customer that is more likely to be attractive.

Customer profiling aggregates data gathered from multiple web sites and allows an online visitor session to be tailored to the unique customer before the potential customer has even identified himself or places an order. Without the business knowing the identity of the site visitor, the business's profiling application can know about this visitor's interests and needs. This is based on identification (ID) information automatically supplied to the business when the visitor arrives on a site. The site is then configured to appeal to the buying habits of that customer. This previously obtained information from other sites is provided without access to the customer's identity, thereby ensuring that privacy rules and best practice are maintained at all times.

Customer-centric e-business

Developing an integrated, customer-centric e-business proposition requires an in-depth understanding of what *your* customer requires from their online relationship with you. Part of the process in achieving this includes using personalization technology to profile (present), match and recommend the right content to the right individual. Let's have a look at each of these in turn.

Step 1: Presentation

The first step is to understand what type of content visitors can view by looking at their browser capabilities, operating system environment and the language of their browser. Once you know these characteristics, you can automatically begin to drive the appropriate content and functionality for each visitor. Have you ever visited a web site and been asked to choose which version of the site you would like to view? Normally, the choices are HTML or Flash versions. Is it best practice to provide the visitor with this choice, or, should the site detect the capabilities of the browser and, if the Flash Player plug-in is presented, automatically load the Flash version of the site? What do you think?

In answer to the question, it depends on two keys things: (1) what the site is trying to achieve and (2) who the target audience is. If your e-business site is B2B, then keeping clear of Flash-only content would be recommended. However, if you are appealing to the B2C audience and want to showcase certain products, then Flash-elements of content can be desirable, for the interactive qualities it offers.

Look at Hoover below. Hoover manufactures and distributes globally domestic appliances, specifically vacuum cleaners. Here, Hoover's e-business site is both transactional and rich in multimedia content. On entry to the site, you are presented with an option – Flash for a rich, interactive experience, or HTML for a faster, lesser interactive experience.

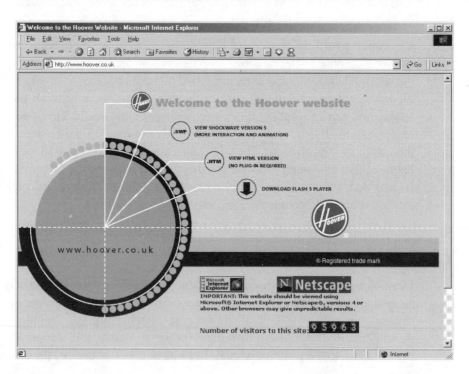

Figure 9.9   The Hoover web site

NOTEPAD EXERCISE

Visit the Hoover web site and make notes on the experience you have with the site. Is this an effective approach for a B2C e-business site?

Step 2: Match

Without requiring a customer to log in to the site, personalization can record the characteristics of content consumed by the visitor and then personalize their experience of the site by adapting navigation and content dynamically, based on their requirements and capabilities. This can help save customers time and increase their satisfaction.

Step 3: Recommendation

The site must use statistical 'predictive' modelling techniques to recommend content and products to a customer based on what we know they are interested in. Increases in customer satisfaction and loyalty can be achieved by increasing the relevance and reliability of individually personalized recommendations for content, products, and services. Other aspects of developing customer-centric e-marketing solutions include using techniques such as 'Personalize this site'. This offers customers an intuitive, browser-based interface to

Figure 9.10   MyYahoo! Personalization from Yahoo!

customize the content, layout and resources of the site, within a roles-based framework set by the site owner, for example My Yahoo! featured here.

This type of 'service' means that customers can be given their own personal workspace within your e-business site that's fully customized to their individual and specific needs. This builds barriers to entry by competitors, reduces the likelihood of customer switching and increases the opportunity for more personalized service and sales. Recent studies, conducted by Mainspring and Bain & Company, show that the average customer must shop four times at an e-business site before the site begins to make profit from that customer. Online businesses must retain a customer for 18 months before they break even! Furthermore, customers will spend increasing amounts of money and refer more shoppers the more often they visit an e-business site. The report also went on to say that spending by an average repeat customer was up 67 percent in their third year of using the site, than in the first six months, and referrals by a customer generally increased fourfold after ten purchases from the site.

9.6 Effective eCRM

Developing effective eCRM should include a mix of redesigning internal business processes, whilst engaging the customer and working with them externally on what they need from the business through the e-business solution. In Figure 9.11, we show where eCRM sits in terms of both new customer acquisition and meeting the ongoing needs of existing customer relationships across whichever channel the customer has chosen to use.

To ensure that eCRM is effective, it should comprise a variety of different aspects, all available via the web browser. We call this the 'browser-based customer service representative' (CSR).

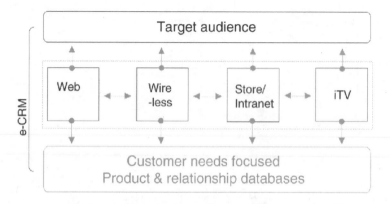

Figure 9.11   eCRM and its role in all channels

Included within the browser-based CSR's armoury, are techniques such as:

- One or two-way e-mail push
- Video push and video streaming to the customer's desktop
- One-way HTML push of specific web pages that the customer may be interested in
- One-way file downloading to the customer's computer, such as demonstration software, video clips, PDF (Adobe Portable Document Format) and Word documents and so on
- One-way white boarding – in order to be able to demonstrate a specific point or highlight a specific feature.

More common techniques of online customer service, seen widely on the web today, are *auto-responders* to incoming e-mail enquiries and call back facilities where the customer can either be contacted on a number they specify at a time they specify, or be connected directly to the CSR via Intelligent Call Routing (ICR).

An ***auto-responder*** is an automated method of delivering information to an e-mail recipient, typically for marketing, customer services or promotional purposes. e-business sites commonly use them when a customer submits an order – the auto-responder sends an e-mail to the customer thanking for the order and confirming its details.

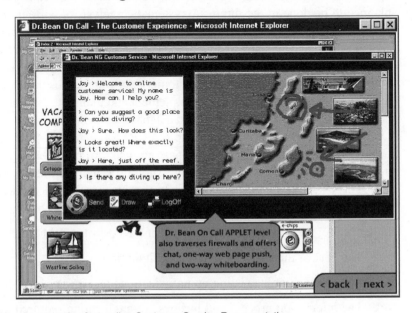

Figure 9.12 – An example of an online Customer Service Representative

All of this is aimed at enhancing the customer relationship and managing customers more effectively, both on and offline.

In Figure 9.12, we picture an example of how an online customer service representative (CSR) can look. The example used is from Dr. Bean (www.drbean.com), demonstrating a number of different online customer service activities taking place. First, the CSR is text-chatting with the customer, and at the same time, white boarding within the customer's browser environment, to highlight a key feature.

9.7 eCRM Return On Investment (ROI)

Calculating the ROI of eCRM is particularly difficult, for three reasons:

1. There is no baseline data prior to the use of the system, making before and after comparison impossible
2. There are too many other independent variables
3. Many benefits are soft or intangible and hard to quantify.

eCRM projects have demonstrated an immediate increase of 8% in revenues and a target growth of 16% within two years.

Before you start to identify areas where cost savings can be made, you will need to estimate the change between how you do things now and how they are planned to be done in the future. A systematic analysis of current operations will produce a detailed baseline from which to measure improvements. The cost of eCRM will depend on the project scope and your existing infrastructure. Costs per customer can vary from as little as £600 to in excess of £8,000. Historically, large-scale back-end customer data warehouses based on legacy technology have been expensive to implement and maintain. However, recent developments in operating system and database technology have dramatically reduced the overall cost of ownership of eCRM systems. At Microsoft, Bill Gate's view of eCRM is that the database application should be a commodity item and data warehousing technology should be included at no additional cost. This will have a significant impact on an e-business's choice of a preferred eCRM platform.

In the future, the key trends that will affect the cost of eCRM are:

- The cost of the software and its configuration
- An organization's existing communications and legacy infrastructure
- The integration process and business re-engineering required as project scopes becomes more ambitious

- The availability of skills and resources in eCRM
- Political and cultural changes to the way eCRM-led organizations handle customer data, privacy and permission.

9.8 Extending your net – a quick insight into extranets

In e-business, B2B and B2C, much of the discussion has been centred around developing web sites that are publicly accessible by customers. However, there exists another channel to market that is proving to be a fundamental enabler of true e-business – the *extranet*.

An *extranet* is a private business environment that uses the Internet as the backbone for communication, commerce and collaboration. Extranets allow organizations to extend mission-critical resources over the Internet to partners, suppliers, customers and 'other' individuals outside the physical walls of the organization.

As markets consolidate, business services are becoming externalized to outside partners, suppliers, outsourcers and consultants. This demands that e-businesses provide a secure, robust and IP (Internet Protocol)-based solution that offers accessibility to these business services. Extranets are the key. Like any aspect of e-business, deploying an extranet requires a deep understanding of internal business processes and external supplier, partner and customer needs. Extranets enable organizations to deploy business intelligence to partners and allow them to access information and applications over the Internet. Extranets can replace a variety of tactical, disparate information-sharing methods, such as telephones, faxes, e-mails and couriers/postal services.

THE KEY BENEFITS OF AN EXTRANET

1. Extranets facilitate greater collaboration between partners, offering the potential for increased revenue through facilitating easier purchasing methods.

2. Extranets provide organizations with improved management of information, resources and applications, facilitating cost reductions and improved efficiencies.

3. Extranets win customers and ensure they keep coming back by offering value.

Extranets are fundamentally changing how companies share internal resources and interact with the outside world. They are built with technology, but used by people. Extranets are not solely developed to reduce costs in communication and information sharing, but to make users feel important and part of the organization, which keeps them coming back and ensures revenue keeps increasing. According to e-business research firm Computer Economics, 78 percent of companies that have deployed extranets experience full or positive returns. Furthermore, Forrester Research predicts that by 2003 extranets will dominate trade, which reinforces the idea that extranets are the foundation of e-business. Companies are no longer asking "Should we build an extranet?" but "How do we build an extranet that gives us a competitive edge?" Companies that have successfully deployed extranets include Kodak, who provide their global retail network with access to an online purchasing system for product and Heineken, who through their HOPS extranet, accepts over 80% of its resellers' orders by enabling them to log-in and place orders.

USEFUL WEB SITES   Referenced in this chapter

Nature Publishing	www.nature.com
First Active Financial (now Britannic Money)	www.britannicmoney.com
Dr Bean	www.drbean.com
Yahoo	www.yahoo.com
Mainspring	www.mainspring.com
Bain & Company	www.bain.com
CareerJournal.com	www.careerjournal.com
Hoover	www.hoover.com

CHAPTER SUMMARY

In this chapter, you have learnt:

1. That eCRM is critical to e-business success in retaining customers and improving satisfaction.

2. That developing an eCRM strategy requires e-businesses to use three key steps: 1. Identify your most profitable customers; 2. Personalize your communications and 3. Evaluate your results.

3. That effective customer data capture can be achieved using online forms, surveys and focus groups and that this leads to building better customer profiles.

4. That analysing customer data acquired from multiple sources is critical to identifying patterns in customer behaviour that can be used to deliver further personalized services.

5. That personalization combines technology and customer information to deliver tailored electronic content to individual customers.

6. That eCRM involves sophisticated services being delivered via the Internet such as call centres guiding the customer through the web site and 'pushing' information to the user instead of relying on the user to 'pull' information.

7. That Extranets are private business environments designed to use the Internet as a vehicle for commerce and collaboration. Extranets will be a critical part of any organization's e-business strategy as they offer cost reductions and an opportunity to enhance long-term customer loyalty and value.

TEST YOURSELF

1. The term eCRM stands for extensive Customer Relationship Management. *True or false?*

2. Integrating eCRM into your e-business strategy can reduce customer attrition by 10% and increase profitability by 20%. *True or false?*

3. eCRM should seek to work across all customer communications platforms. *True or false?*

4. Customers are prepared to pay for the cost of eCRM by receiving enhanced, information-rich personalized relationships. *True or false?*

5. Extranets are perceived to be critical to the development of an e-business strategy. *True or false?*

Chapter **10**

Permission and one-to-one marketing

OVERVIEW

This chapter introduces permission marketing – now one of the hottest topics on the Internet. It also explores the current changes taking place in legislation to protect customers from junk email and outlines the benefits of treating customers as individuals through one-to-one marketing. We've also included an interesting case study in this chapter from online dating agency (permission marketing site) 2busy2surf.com, which is helping consumers and businesses come together online to create a match in needs fulfilment.

LEARNING OBJECTIVES

In this chapter you will learn:

- About the current issues with e-marketing

- How *you* develop an online marketing campaign in line with new legislation

- What 'opt-in', 'opt-out' and 'permission-based' marketing are

- About current and new legislation, such as the Distance Selling Directive.

Chapter Topic	Specific Learning Objective
10.0 Introduction	To define and understand permission marketing
10.1 Current Issues with e-Marketing	The Distance Selling Directive and five ways to build and lose customer trust
10.2 Legislation in e-marketing	How you will be affected by new legislation and what action to take
10.3 Permission-based e-marketing	To understand how to gain customer permission

KEYWORDS

Permission   e-Mail   Legislation   Privacy   Opt-in

10.0 Introduction

The global e-mail marketing industry is set to reach $4.8 billion by 2004, predict analysts at Forrester Research. e-business marketers will take advantage of the e-mail channel by sending out more than 200 billion e-mails to reach their customers, increase their brand visibility and jump-start sales. It is recorded that e-marketers who use e-mail marketing achieve purchase rates of four times higher (with response rates of up to 24% in extreme cases using HTML e-mail) than marketers who continue to use traditional direct mail. However, as the Internet and other digital channels become increasingly more important as vehicles for marketing and selling, so becomes the need to manage customer data more effectively in line with new government rulings.

In this chapter, we will explore the current issues with e-marketing and what new legislation is being put in place to protect customer and consumer personal information. We will also discuss permission-based marketing and the method of developing an effective e-mail-driven marketing relationship with customers.

Permission marketing is an approach to selling goods and services in which a prospect explicitly agrees in advance to receive marketing information.

10.1 Current legal issues with e-marketing

e-Business offers more choice, easier access to products and services and lower prices. It is breaking down trade barriers and opening markets. But some customers are concerned about security of payment, privacy of personal information and how to get redress, should something go wrong in the transaction.

e-Business offers more choice, easier access to products and services and lower prices.

The e-business revolution enables businesses to meet the needs of their customers more precisely. But in turn, it creates concerns about privacy and how data is used and transferred between companies. One of the most significant changes taking place in the marketing environment, affecting both online and offline marketers is the Distance Selling Directive. This was implemented from 4 June 2000, and in summary covers:

- The consumer must be provided with information in a clear and comprehensible manner and in good time before the conclusion of any distance contract.

- The supplier must provide information 'with due regard to the principles of good faith' under the terms of UK law, such as the Unfair Terms in Consumer Contracts Regulations 1994.

- The customer must receive written confirmation of most of the information in 'another durable medium available and accessible to him' by the time of delivery at the latest.

- Customers have the right of withdrawal within seven days or three months (cooling off period)

- The supplier site must reimburse the customer within 30 days from date of contract.

As you can see from this, direct selling on the Internet and through other channels is changing and the e-marketer must be prepared for these changes.

Ignorance is no excuse!

But how do you build that level of trust with customers, to enable you to market and sell online to them?

5 ways to build customer trust through e-business

Building trust online takes effort. Only by consistently performing well in the following ways will you gain your customers' trust, loyalty and advocacy to refer you on.

1. **Leverage your brand** – the values you stand for offline will need to apply online. Make sure these are communicated clearly through your e-marketing communications. See Chapter 4 for more on online branding.

2. **Provide a high quality of experience** through your site – customers will use different touch-points to your brand. That's to be expected. Make sure their experience across every touch-point is the same. See Chapter 8 for more on Quality of Experience.

3. **Deliver on time, every time** – no one likes to be let down and the instant gratification nature of the Internet applies equally online. Customer expectations are enhanced – make sure you can meet them.

4. **Leverage third party brands and logos** – create partnerships and relationships with other important e-business brands. This will ensure that even the most youthful of brands will gain credibility.

5. **Use CRM technology** to ensure you harness the power of the customer profile – information is power, but it's only as good as the application it can be used for. Too much data can be as destructive as too little data. Plan your customer profiling carefully. See Chapter 9 for more on CRM.

5 ways to lose customer trust through e-business

Destroying the relationship online is very easy to do. With threats such as ease of customer switching and increased competition to deal with, getting it wrong is the last thing you want. Avoid the following ways to lose your customers:

1. **Revealing your customer's personal information** to the public through insecure systems will certainly not win you friends, as some of the biggest brands have found, including the consumers' association, Which?;

2. **Allowing hackers to place credit card orders** using fraudulent cards;

3. **Failing to deliver goods** on time having set an expectation with the customer;

4. **Over contacting the customer** through several different channels with the same message;

5. **Over charging customers** for your products / services or shipping costs.

10.2 Legislation in e-marketing

There are a variety of new rulings on distance selling that will have major implications for the e-business. Sales procedures and documentation (including where appropriate web site terms and conditions) will need to be reviewed to ensure they comply with the new laws, which came into effect in June 2000.

Background

The Consumer Protection (Contracts Concluded by Means of Distance Communication) Regulations 2000 will bring into force the European Directive on Distance Selling. The Regulations will apply to most business sectors (one notable exception being financial services, for which separate rules are in the pipeline). They will affect the way businesses are able to market and sell their goods and services to consumers by mail order, over the Internet or by phone.

What types of transaction will be affected?

The scope of the Regulations is very broad, covering contracts for both goods and services concluded by mail order, telephone or over the Internet ('distance contracts'). They do not apply to Business-to-Business (B2B) transactions.

What are the new requirements?

Suppliers will be obliged to provide the consumer with certain minimum information about the product or services, the transaction and the consumer's right to cancel the contract. Failure to provide the requisite information before the contract is made could result in the supplier being unable to enforce the contract.

One of the most important changes introduced by the new Regulations is the consumer's right to cancel a distance contract within a specified "cooling off" period. Failure to inform the consumer of this right will not only make the contract unenforceable, but could also result in fines for the e-business (and in some cases, its Directors or Managers). Where the consumer exercises the right to cancel the agreement, the supplier must reimburse the consumer with any money paid within 30 days (subject to the cost of return postage in the case of goods). The new cancellation rights will not apply in every case. For example, contracts for customized goods, or those that deteriorate rapidly, and contracts for the supply of video or audio recordings or computer software that is unsealed by the consumer are among those excluded from the cancellation provisions.

Suppliers will generally be obliged to fulfil orders within 30 days (unless a different period has been agreed) failing which the consumer will have the right to a refund.

Unsolicited e-mail, faxes and automated calls

The Regulations will restrict the use of unsolicited faxes and automatic calling systems for distance selling purposes, unless the consumer has consented to be contacted by the supplier in that way (permission).

The Regulations will also attempt to tackle the problem of unsolicited e-mail. In its recent consultation, the UK Government has put forward two alternatives: The first is the 'opt-out' system (along the lines of the existing Telephone Preference Service) enabling consumers to avoid 'junk' e-mail by registering with a central register – electronic Mail Preference Service. This will involve additional expense for e-marketers, who will need to consult the list and update their customer lists regularly. The second is the 'opt-in' scheme, enabling subscribers to register their wish to receive such communications. Arguments in favour of this approach include possible savings for recipients and ISPs (Internet Service Providers), who bear the costs of such e-mails, and advantages to businesses in terms of a 'self-selected' audience.

Fraudulent use of payment cards

The Regulations will entitle a consumer to request cancellation of fraudulent payments made using his or her credit or debit card. The Government has sought the industry's views on whether 'virtual cash', for example, electronic purses, should be covered by these provisions, and whether consumers should be responsible for the first £50 of any loss (as permitted by current consumer credit legislation) where cards are used fraudulently in distance transactions.

What action should you take?

The Government is still considering the results of its recent consultation, so the final form of the Regulations is yet to be confirmed. In the meantime, however, all businesses engaged in mail order, online or telephone sales should review their sales and marketing procedures, together with any documentation in anticipation of the proposed changes.

10.3 Permission-based e-marketing

Much of the marketing conducted on the Internet today is mistargeted and misdirected. There was a time when banner advertising was one of the most successful ways to promote or advertise a product, service, web site or brand. Today, banner ads see less than 0.05% response, on average. The issue is that regular web users have become 'banner-blind' - so over-exposed to seeing banner ads at the top of the page, along the side (in button form) or along the bottom of the browser window, that they now just ignore them.

Enter permission-based marketing. Invented by Seth Godin, Yahoo!'s Internet Marketing pioneer, Seth suggests that with over 40 million commercial web sites on the Internet and only 125 million regular surfers with the average seeing over 3,000 advertising messages every day, that there must be a more effective way of marketing to customers who are interested in what you have to offer.

Permission-based marketing seeks to build trust and involve your customers by putting them in control of asking you to keep them informed on information and offers that they are interested in specifically. This is achieved either through working with one of the permission-based marketing sites on the web, such as 2Busy2Surf.com, or by using your site to capture customers 'opt-in' address information. The objective is to gain permission from visitors to your web site to keep them informed, by e-mail, SMS, WAP or through offline channels, on a regular basis of things they have stated they are interested in. This way, instead of trying to sell to them via banners or misplaced advertisements, you can sell to them what you know they want when you have it available.

For example, lets suggest that you are the e-marketing Manager of the Alchemy Insurance Company. By implementing permission-based marketing, you will capture the address information of visitors to alchemyinsures.com and ask them when approximately their insurance expires and by which method of communication they would prefer to hear from you. Having captured this data, you will then hold it within the database until the time comes to contact the prospective customer with an offer of insurance that we know meets their needs. The delivery of this best deal offer will confirm with the rules of 'permission-marketing', as it will be personalized, specific in nature, timely and relevant. But above all, the communication will state that the customer requested the information by this means and will provide the customer with an 'opt-out mechanism' if they no longer wish to be contacted by the Alchemy Insurance Co.

What this has achieved is a far more accurately targeted marketing message to a recipient we know has a need, is already warm to buy and is more likely to action our message than ignore it. The delivery of the marketing message could be by e-mail, which also means that it will have a hyperlink to the correct page on the Alchemy Insurance Co. web site. All in all, a far more pleasing experience for the customer and a far more cost-effective method of customer acquisition for the Alchemy Insurance Co.

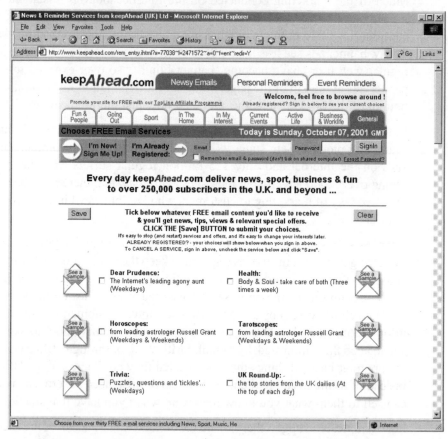

Figure 10.1 Keep Ahead.com's web site where consumers can subscribe to 'permission' e-mail lists on subjects of their choice.

CASE STUDY: 2BUSY2SURF.COM

2busy2surf.com is a business-to-consumer (B2C) web-based service that intelligently matches consumer demand to business supply. The main proposition to consumers is save time, i.e. 2busy2surf.com does the work for you. 2busy2surf.com was established as a company in July 1999, before Seth Godin's widely read book and accepted term 'Permission Marketing' was introduced. Created as a web site where consumers could register their interest in receiving offers by e-mail for specified products, the concept was driven by the desire to put the consumer in control of the information they received.

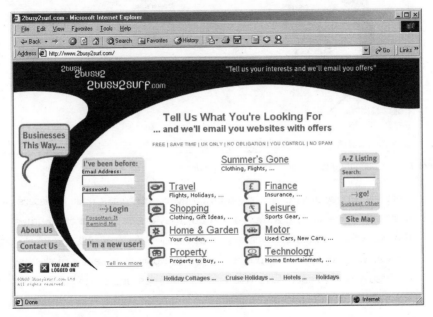

Figure 10.2   2busy2surf.com's web site

At the time of writing (September 2001), Europe is about to pass legislation that will make opting in to e-mail lists a prerequisite for e-mail marketers. This will help to reduce the amount of unsolicited commercial e-mail (UCE) sent, but is still not as thorough as the gold standard of double opt-in. 2busy2surf.com use double opt-in registration ('the second yes') where a user must confirm their e-mail address. Double opt-in e-mail marketing lists are the most effective way of making sure you truly have permission and are honouring your users' wishes.

2busy2surf.com also guarantee never to pass on a registrant's details to third parties for e-mailing of unsolicited communications, another

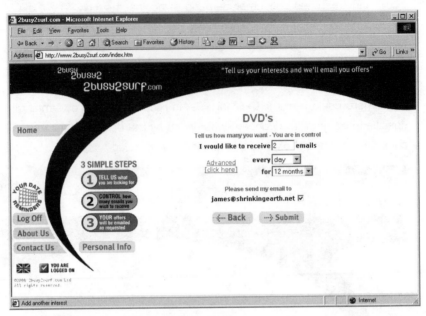

PERMISSION AND ONE-TO-ONE MARKETING

essential element to gaining users' permission and building trust. All e-mails are sent from 2busy2surf.com, again helping to build trust with users.

Figure 10.3   Configuring your profile on 2busy2surf.com

Uniquely, 2busy2surf.com date stamps every interest a user registers, so that rather like turning a tap on and off, they are in control at all times of the flow of e-mail communications they receive. As a result, the whole site acts as one big opt-in tick box, as users are only ever sent e-mails they have specifically requested. This again reinforces users trust in the 2busy2surf.com brand and service.

Users receive e-mails from 2busy2surf.com, which they can view at their leisure and are invited to click a link through to the business's web site if the offer interests them.

Honesty and transparency are also key to building trust online and in this self service environment 2busy2surf.com give users access to their personal information held on the site, which they are free to edit and remove at will. Again users are in control at all times.

As a user registers for different interests with 2busy2surf.com they build up their own unique account or profile of 'current interests', which they are free to edit or cancel. This helps to build 2busy2surf.com's permission marketing and one to one (1:1) marketing approach. As a

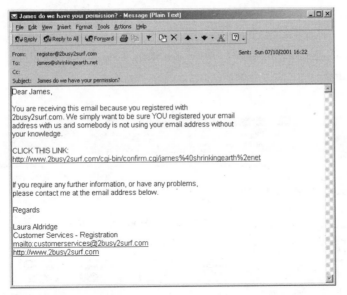

Figure 10.4   e-Mail from 2busy2surf.com

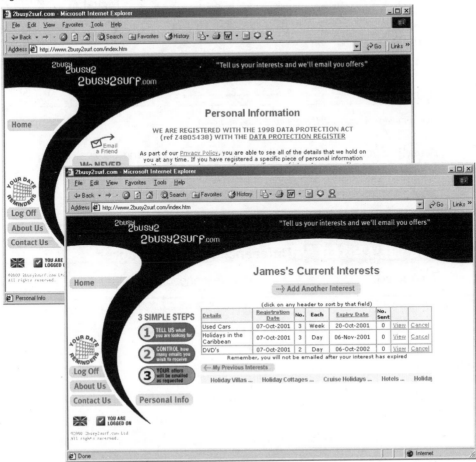

Figure 10.5   Person2busy2surf.com's web site

'virtual' company, 2busy2surf.com enables registered businesses to create e-mails online for their offers. 2busy2surf.com's administration team approve these offers, which are then e-mailed to those consumers who have requested those specific products.

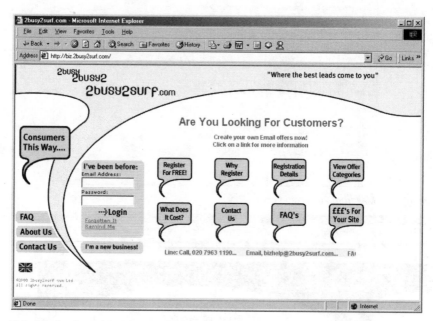

Figure 10.6   Finding the right customers @ 2busy2surf.com

2busy2surf.com is a simple 'dating agency' concept and service, acting as a custodian of consumer data delivering targeted communications by email for offers from pre-qualified businesses.

USEFUL WEB SITES Referenced in this chapter

Keep Ahead	www.keepahead.com
2busy2surf	www.2busy2surf.com
Seth Godin	www.permission.com

CHAPTER SUMMARY

In this chapter, you have learnt:

1. That permission marketing is based on gaining a customer's explicit approval to send them targeted, timely and specific marketing messages.

2. That developing a customer trust in e-marketing requires five key stages: 1. Leverage your brand; 2. Providing a high quality of experience through all channels; 3. Delivering on time, every time; 4. Leveraging third party relationships and logos; 5. Through eCRM.

3. That losing customer trust can be achieved by: 1. Revealing your customer's personal information to the public Internet; 2. By allowing hackers to place fraudulent credit card orders; 3. By failing to deliver goods on time, every time; 4. By contacting your customer with duplicate messages through multiple channels; 5. By over-charging your customers for their products, services or shipping costs.

4. That several new pieces of legislation are currently being developed to include permission-based e-marketing, such as the European Distance Selling Directive, the Data Protection Act and the electronic Mail Preference Service.

5. That permission marketing is designed to replace interruption marketing such as banner advertising and pop-ups, by ensuring customers only see adverts that are relevant, timely and specific to their needs.

6. That sites such as keepahead.com and 2busy2surf.com now exist to provide businesses and consumers with a 'digital dating agency' by bringing together interested prospects and organizations that offer a product or service that meets their needs.

7. That the only way to be successful in permission-based marketing, on or offline, is to ensure you offer your customers and prospects complete honesty and transparency in the relationship.

TEST YOURSELF

1. Permission marketing is the process of selling goods or services in which a prospect explicity agrees to receive marketing messages. *True or false?*

2. Permission-based e-mail marketing in HTML format can increase response rates to as much as 24%. *True or false?*

3. Revealing your customer's personal information publicly on the Internet is one of five ways you can build trust. *True or false?*

4. Permission-based marketing is based on ensuring marketing messages are personalized, specific in nature, timely and relevant. *True or false?*

5. To utilize permission marketing, you need your own customer database. *True or false?*

Chapter **11**

**e-Business
case studies**

OVERVIEW

This chapter looks at particular companies and their use of e-business. We will look in detail at RS Components, figleaves.com and boo.com to see their use of e-marketing, customer care and their achievements

LEARNING OBJECTIVES

In this chapter you will learn about:

- A major business-to-business brand that has successfully developed and implemented e-business and e-marketing campaigns

- A major business-to-customer brand that has successfully developed and implemented e-business and e-marketing campaigns

- Lessons you can learn to avoid a .com disaster.

Chapter Topic	Specific Learning Objective
11.0 Introduction	
11.1 RS Components	A business-to-business case study
11.2 figleaves.com	A business-to-customer case study
11.3 boo.com	How to avoid a .com disaster

KEYWORDS

Business-to-business (B2B)   Business-to-customer (B2C)

11.0 Introduction

Throughout this book, we have discussed various best practice techniques in e-business and e-marketing. But amongst all the noise of the Internet and other digital channels, who is doing these things well? Additionally, if you are about to develop your e-business strategy, what lessons can be learned and implemented? In this final chapter, we will attempt to answer these questions, as we take a quick peek at why one of Europe's best known fashion e-tailers, boo.com was so unsuccessful, whilst others, such as lingerie site figleaves.com continues to grow at 300% per annum.

 11.1 Business-to-Business – RS Components

www.rswww.com is the Internet trading arm of RS Components – a major UK distributor of electro-mechanical components with a vision to establish itself as 'a serious place to do business that makes technical users successful'.

SOME FACTS ABOUT RSWWW.COM (UK)

RS sell through various channels, to include:

- Print Catalogue – featuring 130,000 products, produced and distributed twice per year

- CD-ROM – as above but with greater content depth (primarily technical information) and interactivity – hybrid functionality links user to the web for online purchasing

- Call centre – fully integrated with all other sales channels

- 13 Trade counters

Customers

rswww.com's customers incorporate many diverse groups including companies of all sizes, from sole traders to huge multinationals. Most customers fall into the medium-sized company segment. The individuals who order from rswww.com include purchasing managers, electronic or electrical engineers and mechanics. Online order values across all customer segments are an average of £81, but volumes are high. Orders are occasionally received for amounts close to £10,000 from larger customers.

Why do e-business?

RS Components decided to establish an Internet trading channel for several reasons, including:

- A customer willingness to switch to an electronic medium;

- An opportunity to enhance their already impressive service offering to customers;

- To take advantage of an opportunity to enable rapid, profitable growth world-wide;

- To counter competitive threats.

The evolution of RS's e-business strategy took place over a period of three years. In 1997, a working prototype of the site was developed to demonstrate the potential of the Internet to board members. This was done to gain management buy-in and secure funding for the project. In the early stages of 1998, phase 1 of the web site was launched, closely followed by phase 2 later in the year, seeing more functionality being added. During 2000, further enhancements were implemented, seeing the site integrate with an eCommerce portal and an e-Procurement service.

What were RS's e-business objectives?

RS had a number of different objectives for their Internet trading channel. These included:

- Creating a reliable and robust Internet trading channel;

- Guaranteeing next-day delivery for all online orders received up to 8pm that working day;

- To provide world-class technical support for customers;

- To deliver online ordering services that satisfy user purchasing needs;

- To make purchasing online easier and more intuitive to use;

- To increase savings to the customer from using the online trading channel.

The web site developed by RS offers impressive personalized services to customers and delivers cost savings by streamlining the order process, cutting out previously necessary paperwork and providing controls that empower end-users to order online. Following customer feedback and learning curve improvements, the web site offers the following benefits to customers:

- A good standard of usability and intuitive navigation;

- A personalized service supported by customer, technical data and product databases;

- Stock level enquiries through an hourly batch link to the product inventory system;

- Historical reporting to check order history over the preceding 13 months;

- Purchasing controls that allow purchasing managers to cut out several layers of paperwork in processing high volume, low value orders. This results in cost savings of as much as 84 per cent of the cost of the ordering process;

- Price information is personalized to the customer by showing price breaks available for volume purchases;

- Information on discontinued lines and alternative products;

- Technical information, previously only available in office hours through the call centre, is now available in the Infozone;

- Order confirmation.

Databases

RS's e-business is fully integrated with three database systems:

- Technical information database: the Infozone, containing technical documents provided 24 hour, seven-days a week technical support on all the products featured in the rswww.com catalogue;

- Catalogue database: information about the product range;

- Customer database, including all registered user and customer contact details, purchase history and promotion history.

Customers need to register personal information before they can purchase on the site. RS now have over 300,000 users who have registered on the web site. Reporting and tracking functionality allow customers' movements around the site to be monitored and reports generated showing visits, registrations, sales volume and value.

11.2 Business-to-Consumer – figleaves.com

figleaves.com is Europe's leading online underwear retailer, with turnover rising sixfold between 2000 and 2001, and expected to quadruple this year. Its proposition to consumers is based on three promises – **selection**, **simplicity** and **satisfaction** – and the end-to-end experience is designed to make the shopping experience as pain free as possible. Whether customers want a simple, anonymous shop or hands-on personal help, they can find it at figleaves.com.

SOME QUICK FACTS ABOUT FIGLEAVES.COM

- 90% of sales are in the UK but they also sell around the world

- figleaves.com have developed an integrated, end-to-end e-tailing solution, from web site to warehouse.

- Although e-business permeates all of their systems, it is only one of their sales channels.

- Around 20% of figleaves.com orders are placed by phone and a further 20% are catalogue influenced.

- Supplier relationships are seen as strategic. Suppliers are treated as if they had a concession in a department store and micro sites are developed for each brand.

- A global network of small warehouses, controlled centrally, enables them to provide high quality delivery services to customers.

Figure 11.1 – Figleaves.com – The home page of their e-business site

---

KEY ISSUES FACED

Here are some of the key issues faced by figleaves.com in becoming the world's leading lingerie e-tailer.

- Maintaining operational excellence;

- Continuing to drive sales growth linked to addressable market size;

- The successful launch of the T-bra, personal measurement device;

- Successful launch in the USA – a hard market to crack for any e-tailer.

Selection

Product choice is crucial to the figleaves.com proposition. It offers everything from the Aristoc to Zimmerli of underwear – an unrivalled selection of over 70 brands, and is the exclusive online and catalogue stockist for some leading brands. They site offers over 10,000 different items and aim to have over 95% in stock, carrying all sizes from every range.

Simplicity

The figleaves.com proposition is 'shop the way you want to shop'. It allows consumers to shop by brand, using finders, bestsellers, fashion recommendations, etc. The process is made painless by asking consumers five simple questions and then matching the answers provided to all products in the web site database. The web site design is geared towards ease of use, rather than fancy, time-consuming graphics.It also shows real-time stock levels and allows customers to place items on back-order, should the product be temporarily out of stock. Customers who order out of stock items automatically receive a £5 voucher off their next purchase in appreciation of their patience.

Satisfaction

All in-stock goods are despatched the same day (as long as the order is received by 4pm. Delivery is free and figleaves.com offer a no quibble, free returns policy. Customers' credit cards are only charged when the goods have left the building. figleaves.com aims to acknowledge returns by e-mail within 24 hours and confirm that money has been refunded or goods replaced. They keep good contact with their customers. For instance, figleaves.com will e-mail a customer with a status report if it is waiting for items from manufacturers. The web site also carries its address and phone numbers, as well as a customer services email address so that customers can have confidence in being able to contact them. Simple, even basic, but incredibly important in ensuring the business is accessible to customers.

figleaves.com have invested significantly in developing a state of the art warehouse management system, incorporating 'pick by lights' radio technology and custom gift-wrap stations. This is fully integrated with customer-facing systems, allowing automatic confirmation of order dispatch and progressing of self-checking of order status by customer enquiry. The system significantly improves figleaves.com's ability to combine high quality distribution, both in terms of speed and accuracy, with high quality product offered by the brands.

Overall, buying from figleaves.com is as pain-free as online shopping can be. They have invested heavily on back office functions, rather than high profile marketing campaigns. A strategy that is paying off! figleaves.com is one of the few e-tailers that is growing at a rate of over 300 per cent per annum and are projecting sales of £4.2 million ($6.3m) this financial year. This is against a backdrop of single digit sales growth among the main ISPs, and failures amongst some of the highest profile clothing and lingerie online retailers.

Customer acquisition

figleaves.com's primary e-marketing activity revolves around the use of an affiliate scheme. It has a presence on 1,400 partner web sites and has 15 key affiliates that it manages in-house. These range from MSN.com to Handbag.com and Virgin.net. Affiliate sales account for approximately 30% of the total sales. They have built this network up by providing them with an editorial and promotional programme and have found regular competitions to be extremely effective in building its customer base. A recent competition to win £400 worth of luxury underwear and tickets for a Tom Jones concert (an obvious connection) on AOL was seen by 130,000 people. Of these, over 18,000 clicked-through to find out more and almost 12,000 of these entered. What's more, over 7,500 entrants joined the figleaves e-mail alert service.

In addition to its online business, figleaves.com recognized the importance of offering alternative channels to to its customers. Last autumn it launched its first print catalogue. This went out to its own customer base as well as through targeted publications, such as Tatler and Red, plus retailers such as French Connection. It succeeded on all three levels. figleaves.com enjoyed a 4% overall response and generated over £250,000 in sales. They now produce two main seasonal catalogues along with Valentines and Christmas flyers and plan to segment with basics and larger sizes brochures in the pipeline.

Keeping customers

Everything figleaves.com do is prompted by a desire to provide the levels of customer service that will engender long-term customer loyalty. As a result, almost 50% of orders are repeat orders. The company has created an ethos where everybody who works for figleaves.com recognizes that customer satisfaction is the ultimate aim.Its customer service desk receives approximately 375 emails a week and all are dealt with within 24 hours of receipt. On average, figleaves.com receives 20 emails of praise each week and one or two complaints. If a customer has had to wait for a late delivery from a brand figleaves.com will, for example, throw in a free pack of briefs or send them a voucher. Likewise, at Christmas it sends personal messages and vouchers to its highest spending customers.

e-Mail marketing

Every week figleaves.com send out around 80,000 e-mails to customers or registered site users who have 'opted in' to receiving them. The e-mails are short and used to inform customers about new products, offers and competitions. They send out a special e-mails to registered site users who have never purchased. These feature special offers not available on the site, and have generated up to 20% of sales in one week. The drop-out rate is less than 1% a month, low compared to the industry average.

Additional services

- figleaves.com provide a gift-wrap option – free on orders over £50.
- they run a 'blame it on us' service for customers who have forgotten important dates, citing a problem at the warehouse. In its first six months it was used 250 times.
- they will also send gifts anonymously, allowing the recipient to reply to the donor via their site. In its first six months it was used 525 times.

In summary

figleaves.com is an e-business that will do whatever it takes to keep its customers happy and coming back. Their approach operates on two levels:

- Having the best and most up-to-date systems in place to ensure an efficient service for customers;
- Providing human, personal customer service at all times and under all circumstances.

figleaves.com is not about impressive media stunts or award-winning TV campaigns. It's about commitment and having customer satisfaction as the driver for every part of the business.

What's next for figleaves.com?

In August 2001, figleaves.com launched in the US market, where they also offer free delivery. Initially this will be through a partnership with AOL. In early 2002, figleaves.com will launch a totally new e-business site containing state of the art, user-friendly innovations. These are currently top-secret, so I can't reveal what these will be – you'll just have to keep checking at the site.

During the latter stages of 2001, they will launch a new bra measuring service, the T-bra, that will enable its customers to accurately measure themselves in the comfort and privacy of their own homes. At the same time, figleaves.com will be measuring all the bras they sell and applying their own sizing system to them. This strategy will ensure women will be able to buy with confidence armed not only with the knowledge of their true size, but also the true size of the various brands and styles. This is part of figleaves.com USP (Unique Selling Point) and will eventually make its way on to the high street.

WORDS OF WISDOM FROM FIGLEAVES.COM

So what can figleaves.com teach you about e-business or offer you in preparation of your own e-business adventure? Well, the following:

1. Ideas are worthless; Execution is everything.

2. Don't believe the laws of business are suspended for an e-business.

3. Recruit fantastic people – 1 excellent person is worth 10 mediocre people.

4. Treat all customers like they are your only customer.

5. Provide excellence in service.

6. Don't think e-business is exclusively about the Internet.

7. Always look to develop additional revenue streams.

A FINAL POINT! EVOUCHER – AN OFFER TO MY READERS

Figleaves.com offers you £10.00/$15.00 off (on a minimum £30.00/ $45.00 spend) eVouchers for buying and/or reading this book. The personalized vouchers for *e-business* readers can be redeemed at **www.figleaves.com/e-business**, or forwarded to your friends, family and colleagues.

11.3 Lessons to be learnt – boo.com

Successful e-businesses, such as Dell, Amazon, RS and figleaves, all have one thing in common – they integrate the customer into the entire interactive relationship process, by providing customer-centric tools and facilities that offer value and enable the relationship to be developed, enhanced and extended. However, we have seen many major .com brands demonstrate how not to do it. The industry is shaking out the weak, the gravy-train riders and those who think they can make a quick buck. The list of .com casualties grows longer by the day and have included big names such as eGarden.com and eToys, amongst many others.

One of the first and probably most valuable .com disasters to take place was boo.com – a privately owned, venture capital funded fashion retail site that managed to spend its way through £100 milllion of someone else's money by employing 400 people to get e-business very wrong.

boo.com demonstrated clearly what happens when you don't have a well-planned, carefully thought-out and well-executed e-business strategy:

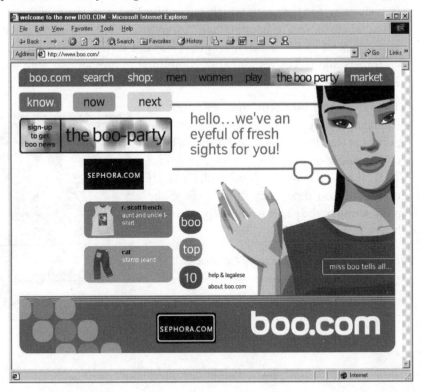

Figure 11.2 – Boo.com re-invents itself

(1) You launch late

Having hyped the site launch with major advertising campaigns on TV, Radio, Billboards and the Press, across Europe and the USA, boo.com launched much later than it stated. This ensured it had already lost credibility with consumers, before it had got off the ground.

(2) You change the proposition overnight

boo.com's 'launch' proposition was high-value, premium branded sports and leisure goods. If you were a boo.com customer, price was not your concern; lifestyle was. Within three months, boo.com had changed its proposition by slashing prices and offering branded goods at upto 40% discount.

(3) You get the web site's technical capabilities wrong

Boo.com was a bloated, over-specified, bandwidth hungry web site that offered slow-to-load 3D rotating product images, lots of flash content and what everyone thought would be its most compelling feature – avatar Miss Boo, the site's online personal shopping assistant, designed to help shoppers spend more of their money. However, whilst a triumph for the techies that had built it, a disaster for the users which left a bitter taste in the mouth and many potential customers re-booting their computers. What boo.com demonstrated was a lack of customer knowledge. It had not tested the site properly with customers and it was certainly not committed to providing a high quality of experience based on the services it had initially said it would offer.

The story of boo.com has become so legendary in the e-business community that publisher Random House is producing a book called *boohoo.com*, due out in November 2001. It promises to be a good read, that is, if it launches on time, they don't change the proposition or the paper isn't too (bandwidth) heavy for readers!

Figure 11.3 – boo.com was snapped up by Fashionmall

For more e-business case studies, visit the book's companion site at
www.bh.com/companions/0750652934

USEFUL WEB SITES	Referenced in this chapter
RS Compnents	rswww.com
figleaves	figleaves.com
boo.com/Fashionmall	fashionmall.com

CHAPTER SUMMARY

In this chapter you have learnt:

1. The difference between business-to-business and business-to-customer companies and the different customer care and marketing techniques involved.

2. The importance of understanding your target customer audience, and whether your company is suitable for e-business.

3. The need for a well-planned business strategy and the research involved to aviod a .com disaster such as boo.com's.

Index